MAKING OF THE

A Study In

FOREWORD BY

University of
Notre Dame

Patrick Romanell

MEXICAN MIND
Recent Mexican Thought

EDGAR S. BRIGHTMAN

Notre Dame Press
London

Reprinted by special arrangement with
Patrick Romanell.

First paperback edition — 1967
UNIVERSITY OF NOTRE DAME PRESS
Notre Dame, Indiana

Second Printing — 1971

First edition — 1952
UNIVERSITY OF NEBRASKA PRESS
Lincoln, Nebraska

Printed in the United States of America
by NAPCO Graphic Arts, Inc., Milwaukee, Wisconsin

To

CORNELIUS KRUSÉ

Inter-American Ambassador of Philosophy

ACKNOWLEDGMENTS

I wish to express my appreciation to Columbia University for the award of a Cutting Traveling Fellowship, and to the Carnegie Endowment for International Peace for a supplementary grant, both of which enabled me to do research in Mexico during the academic year 1945-46 on the theme of this book. At that time I had the pleasure of interviewing practically all the present-day Mexican and Spanish-refugee thinkers to whom I refer in the text, including the late Ezequiel Chávez and the late Antonio Caso. For their generous assistance and cheerful cooperation, I am most deeply grateful.

I also wish to thank my friend Jack Malone of Pittsburgh for his insights into the Mexican Revolution of 1910, my former colleague Miriam Small from Maine for useful information on American folklore, and the French-born painter Jean Charlot for his observations on the Mexican mural movement. My friend Chauncey Leake of Galveston was a constant source of encouragement throughout the whole period of the preparation of the present work.

I am especially indebted to my colleague Edgar S. Brightman of Boston University for writing the spirited Foreword, and to Miss Emily Schossberger of the University of Nebraska Press for using her editorial pencil sparingly but effectively. Of course, I alone am responsible for whatever errors still remain in the text. Words cannot express how much I owe to my wife, who shared with me the countless hours of joy and labor that went into the making of this book.

Mexico City   P.R.
July, 1952

The author is grateful to the following publishers for permission to quote from the sources specified:

CAMBRIDGE UNIVERSITY PRESS, Cambridge, England: Werner Brock, *An Introduction to Contemporary German Philosophy*, 1935.

COLUMBIA UNIVERSITY PRESS, New York: Herbert W. Schneider, *A History of American Philosophy*, 1946.

HENRY HOLT & Co., New York: Henri Bergson, *Creative Evolution*, 1911; *The Two Sources of Morality and Religion*, 1935.

J. B. LIPPINCOTT Co., New York: Gerald W. Johnson, *Our English Heritage*, 1949.

MACMILLAN Co., New York: Henri Bergson, *Laughter*, 1911. Alfred N. Whitehead, *Science and the Modern World*, 1925; *Adventures of Ideas*, 1933; F. S. C. Northrop, *The Meeting of East and West*, 1946; *The Logic of the Sciences and the Humanities*, 1947.

MINTON, BALCH & Co., New York: John Dewey, *Art as Experience*, 1934.

W. W. NORTON & Co., New York: José Ortega y Gasset, *The Modern Theme*, 1933; *Toward a Philosophy of History*, 1941; *Concord and Liberty*, 1946.

OXFORD UNIVERSITY PRESS, New York: John Tate Lanning, *Academic Culture in the Spanish Colonies*, 1940.

PHILOSOPHICAL LIBRARY, New York: Henri Bergson, *The Creative Mind*, 1946.

PRINCETON UNIVERSITY PRESS: José Ortega y Gasset, *Mission of the University*, 1944.

SIMON AND SCHUSTER, INC., New York: Bertrand Russell, *A History of Western Philosophy*, 1945.

UNIVERSITY OF CHICAGO PRESS: Nicholas J. Spykman, *The Social Theory of Georg Simmel*, 1925. José Vasconcelos and Manuel Gamio, *Aspects of Mexican Civilization*, 1926.

YALE UNIVERSITY PRESS: Carl L. Becker, *The Heavenly City of the Eighteenth-Century Philosophers*, 1932; F. S. C. Northrop (ed.), *Ideological Differences and World Order*, 1949.

CONTENTS

CONTENTS

FOREWORD

Professor Patrick Romanell has rendered a conspicuous service to international and intercultural understanding by giving to the English-reading public this reliable account of the Mexican mind. If ever a book was needed, this is the one. Up to now there has been an almost perfect vacuum in the field of English-language books about Mexican thought.

In general, the scholarly world outside the Iberian orbit has been almost as ignorant as the general public about the intellectual life, and especially the philosophical thought, of Latin America. There are, it is true, several reasonably good books about political, economic, social, and religious conditions south of the border. Some novels and essays are available. But almost no information about Latin-American philosophers is to be found in most works of reference. Our dictionaries, encyclopaedias, and histories of philosophy are as barren as the desert when it comes to Latin America. Even the great five-volume Ueberweg—the standard German history of philosophy, which is supposed to tell us something about everyone everywhere in the realm of philosophy—devoted a scant half page of Vol. V of its latest pre-war edition to the whole of Central and South America. The ill-informed writer mentions a few European influences on Ibero-American thought, names two Cuban philosophers (one of whose names is spelled in two variant forms) and no one at all from either Central or South America. This approaches a maximum in scholarly inefficiency. To make the illustration perfect for our purpose, Mexico is not even hinted at.

It is true that Professor William Rex Crawford of the University of Pennsylvania, formerly cultural attaché to our legation in Rio de Janeiro, has provided us with a book, *A Century of Latin-American Thought* (1944), which gives a bird's-eye view of the Latin-American intellectual scene. But it includes *pensadores* who are far from being philosophers in the strict sense and omits many who should have been included. Moreover, it quickly went out of print. It was a useful survey but did not cover any man or country very thoroughly. In recent years the philosophical journals of this country, notably *Philosophy and Phenomenological Research,* have begun to take much more serious notice of Latin-American thought. This interest has been stimulated by three Inter-American Congresses of Philosophy—in Haiti, New York, and Mexico—and a conference at New Haven, not to mention a Congress in Argentina, which was widely boycotted because of the Argentine policy limiting intellectual liberties in the universities.

The Latinos themselves have in the past few years become more keenly aware of the development of their own philosophical thought, which had, for a long time, existed in relatively isolated centers, despite the wide influence of men like Andrés Bello and Eugenio María de Hostos. Of late, men like Samuel Ramos and Leopoldo Zea in Mexico and Guillermo Francovich in Bolivia have been making invaluable historical contributions.

The present work by Professor Romanell is a rich mine of information that is nowhere else available in English. Although widely acquainted with the whole range of Ibero-American thought, he has wisely confined himself to our neighbor, Mexico, where he has spent considerable time in research after his teaching experience at the University of Panama. It is of special importance to the reading public of the United States to understand sympathetically the Mexican mind if any good-neighbor policy is to strike deep roots. We can learn much from his book. Romanell's account of the malignant influence of positivism in supporting the oppressive Díaz regime—an account which has profited by the research of Leopoldo Zea—might well cause contemporary positivists to think twice about the social consequences of a positivistic theory of value, even if the positivism of the Díaz time was theoretically much more appreciative of moral values than is the more recent variety.

Romanell's vivid and frank pictures of Antonio Caso and José Vasconcelos—two great leaders of the 1910 revolt against positivism in Mexico—shed a bright light on the background of twentieth-century Mexico. The author chose well in selecting these two men for special treatment. While each is highly individual, each is also typically Mexican, and at the same time genuinely philosophical in temper. In the death of Caso, the world of culture and democratic social philosophy suffered great loss. Fortunately,

José Vasconcelos is still alive, and continues the friendly visits to the United States which he initiated long ago.

To become acquainted with the thought of Caso and Vasconcelos, to learn something of the active younger minds who are living forces in the philosophy of today's Mexico, to look back at the kind and scholarly Chávez and ahead to the promising future, are refreshing and revealing experiences, especially profitable to one whose education has been molded in the United States. Mexicans approach philosophy from a different tradition, with different emphasis, and (to a certain extent) with different problems from those that are familiar north of the border. Precisely because of the difference in idiom, each should learn from the other. The breeze of Mexican thought that blows through the pages of Professor Romanell's book may well blow away some of ·the dust from the Yankee Academe. The Mexican approach to problems may serve to crowd some of us out of familiar ruts and to give us a new view of the surrounding landscape.

Above all, this book will help us to see Mexico as a land of intellectual culture and vigorous constructive thought. For many of us, Mexico is a place of exotic beauty, rich in antiquities, quaintly foreign, a source of political, social, and economic problems, and doubtless also of brilliant art and music. But it is far more than all that. It is also a land where keen minds wrestle with the ultimate problems which concern all philosophers. Mexico is a state in the republic of letters, a state in which philosophy flourishes. While there is something characteristically Mexican about their philosophy, Mexican thinkers are seekers of universal truth. As José Vasconcelos has dreamed of a cosmic race, so Mexican philosophy has aspired to cosmic truth. This book brings home to its readers the values and the limitations of provincialism in thought, while mirroring at the same time the essential struggle of all philosophy to overcome provincialism.

Provincialism! How difficult it is for us North Americans to eradicate it from our own attitudes. Our country is "God's country." We arrogate to ourselves the very name of "American," which by right belongs to every citizen of North, Central and South America. We call our country "*The* United States," in sublime disregard of the Mexican United States as well as the United States of Venezuela. Americans of the United States of America should be reminded that we are not the only Americans, and that our country is not the only United States. Nor is our culture the only American culture. There will be an enlightening and broadening experience for everyone who becomes acquainted through this book with the scholarly and free philosophical activity which prevails among our American neighbors in the Mexican United States.

EDGAR SHEFFIELD BRIGHTMAN

Boston University

Each life looks at the universe from its own point of view.

José Ortega y Gassett

PREFACE

Twentieth-century philosophy in Mexico, the principal concern of this book, holds quite a unique place in the history of Mexican culture. Even though philosophical activity has been going on in Mexico since at least the sixteenth century, if not before, it is only in the last forty years or so that the pursuit of philosophy has achieved the status of independence in that picturesque land. Prior to the present century, philosophy in Mexico and, for that matter, throughout Latin America in general, was at the service of either the church, state, school, or industry. With philosophy playing the antiquated rôle of the handmaiden, it is obvious that no development of the Mexican mind on the philosophical plane could have been possible. For there can't be any *Mexican* philosophy, strictly speaking, unless first there is *philosophy* in the genuine sense of critical reflection. The present volume taken as a whole confirms this conclusion.

It is natural that the independent status recently acquired in Mexico by philosophy as a discipline should have been accompanied by a rather intense urge on the part of contemporary Mexican thinkers to look at themselves *as Mexicans.* This makes intelligible the prevalence, in current discussions, of the cultural theme of the Mexican mind, the American mind, and the two Americas. Incidentally, the corresponding theme prevails here with us, though I think for quite a different reason, the explanation of which would lead us too far afield. Nonetheless, it is enough to note in this regard the recent publications of such books as *Characteristically American* by a Harvard philosopher and *The American Mind* by a Columbia historian. At any rate, the fact that the first appearance in English of the versatile Mexican writer Alfonso Reyes is a selection of his essays on the theme in question, published in this country about a year ago under the title of *The Position of America,* is itself evidence of the growing interest among us in knowing how the other side of the Rio Grande feels and thinks.

Before some of the present-day Mexican thinkers are allowed to speak for themselves concerning their particular cast of mind and its difference from ours, in the introductory chapter I shall attempt to do the same thing in my own terms. It should be added that the character sketch presented there of the two Americas, an abridged form of which was discussed at a session of the Third Inter-American Congress of Philosophy held at Mexico City in January of 1950, is not written merely out of pure intellectual curiosity. It is motivated by a desire to show that we do not further the *understanding* of the spirit of the other America by a *misunderstanding* of our own. In other words, at the risk of uttering a truism, it takes understanding *of,* as well as *on,* both sides to reach an intercultural *rapprochement,* let alone put a Good Neighbor Policy into practice. My attendance at the East-West Philosophers' Conference held at the University of Hawaii in the summer of 1949 only served to reinforce on a wider scale this conviction of mine.

As to the character sketch itself, it is perhaps only novel in terminology. It happens that I prefer aesthetic categories to other kinds in distinguishing between the Anglo-American attitude towards life and the Ibero-American, namely, "the *epic* sense of life" and "the *tragic* sense of life," respectively. The latter phrase, of course, has been borrowed from the Spanish existentialist Miguel de Unamuno. The former I have coined for the sake of contrast, but it could have easily come, if it actually hasn't, from the pen of the North American pragmatist William James. In fact, interestingly enough, our characteristically North American philosopher *par excellence* saw the world, to use his own words in the classic book entitled *Pragmatism,* "as something more epic than dramatic." James the pragmatist, to quote again from the same book, lived in an "epic kind of a universe." On the other hand, it can be appropriately said that the Mexican painter José Clemente Orozco, who is as characteristically Hispano-American as William James is typically Anglo-American, lived in a tragic or dramatic kind of universe.

My next chapter is historical in content, but its aim is merely to supply enough background to show how the Mexican mind arrived at its present stage of self-awareness. It distinguishes five stages in the story of Mexican thought, emphasizing the bearings of the Mexican Revolution of 1910 upon the making of the Mexican mind. These bearings have been so important in the intellectual life of contemporary Mexico that the rest of the book deliberately concentrates on those men who have given impetus to the nationalistic current of thought stemming from the Revolution. This explains why other thinkers and philosophical movements have received little or no attention in the present work.

The two chapters that follow deal with the most systematic makers of the Mexican philosophical mind since the Revolution, Antonio Caso and José Vasconcelos. Both of these men reflect in their philosophical thought the direct influence of Bergson in Mexico, not to mention the indirect influence of a much earlier Frenchman, Blaise Pascal. Caso's "Christian vision of the world" works out the dualistic strain in the Bergsonian philosophy, Vasconcelos' "aesthetic monism" the mystical. Antonio Caso will always be remembered in Mexico as the first dean of Mexican philosophy. And if one is looking for originality in Ibero-American philosophy, the place to find it, I believe, is in Vasconcelos. The system of Aesthetic Monism, to be sure, suffers from the defects of its qualities, but its peculiar insights into the metaphysical significance of art may help us attain a more well-rounded philosophy of life.

Just as the chapter on Caso and the one on Vasconcelos reveal how influential Henri Bergson was in the immediate past of Mexico, so the final chapter on the latest trends in Mexican philosophical thought point to the even greater influence of José Ortega y Gasset. It is originally through the "perspectivism" of this living Spanish philosopher that the generation of Mexican intellectuals after Caso and Vasconcelos who were inspired by the Mexican Revolution of 1910 to look at the world from a *Mexican* point of view acquired the conceptual means to do so. In addition, it is primarily through Ortega's extraordinary efforts as editor and publisher that contemporary German philosophy was first introduced into the Spanish-speaking countries. This double influence of Ortega's—as perspectivist and promulgator of German thought—continues in Mexico at the moment via a Spanish-refugee group of intellectuals, Juan David García Bacca and José Gaos in particular. And, according to all reports, it is getting stronger. A glance at the issues of the Mexican quarterly *Filoso-*

fía y Letras within the last five years will disclose at once how strong the Orteguian influence is in Mexico today.

To cite the latest examples of its manifestations that have come to my attention since the completion of this book, I have been informed that the National University of Mexico is to publish a large "History of Ideas in Mexico" written by various specialists. Moreover, there is a new group, "Hiperión" by name, of young Mexican students who have come under the influence of German and French existentialism, and whose ambition is to utilize existentialist concepts for a concrete description of the Mexican himself. Another example is the recent publication of a small volume on aesthetics, *Filosofía de la vida artística,* by the Mexicanist Samuel Ramos. Its orientation is essentially existentialist, the method used being that of Moritz Geiger's "phenomenological aesthetics." And finally, a Spanish edition of Martin Heidegger's much-discussed but little-read treatise, *Sein und Zeit,* translated by José Gaos, has just been published in Mexico City with the title of *El ser y el tiempo*—an editorial feat if ever there was one!

So much for the subject matter of the present volume. A few words about the mode of presentation. To facilitate reading, there are no page-by-page footnotes; the references to each chapter have been put at the end. The translations of quoted material are mine unless otherwise specified. The bibliography is limited to books and pamphlets in the field of recent Mexican thought; other materials consulted, including articles from journals, are listed under the chapter references. I regret that the most recent publications in the bibliography reached me too late to be incorporated in the body of the text.

1

A Character Sketch of
the two Americas

A people's philosophy is something quite different from a philosopher's philosophy. The first, according to one of our historians, "is not bound between covers. It is no respecter of logical systems. It is a vast complex of memories, prejudices, inclinations and emotions with which the discipline of the schools has little to do."[1] As to how the two types may be connected, it was Whitehead who discerned that "every philosophy is tinged with the colouring of some secret imaginative background, which never emerges explicitly into its trains of reasoning."[2] To inquire, therefore, into the philosophy the great majority of a people live under from day to day is to search for that secret imaginative background behind the ideas which their professional thinkers entertain concerning human life. This search is much needed at the present moment of international conflict.

If social inquiry is to resolve our intercultural problems on a theoretical plane, it must trace them back to their psychological roots before men of action can be expected to cope with them intelligently. To do so means to uncover the unwritten philosophies of the peoples involved. It does not mean, however, what Professor Northrop advances with unusual conviction in *The Meeting of East and West,* namely, "a determination of the differing ideological assumptions of the major peoples and cultures"[3] in the contemporary world. For the ideological assumptions of a given culture, constituting on formulation the written philosophy of that culture, are not its *roots,* but the general theoretical expression of its *fruits.* Granting that it is by its fruits that the roots of a culture are eventually known, still we should not identify the two poles of the situation. In other words, we should not put last things first. Consequently, to carry through Northrop's timely proposal of tracing our ideological tensions back to their roots, two things must be done. One is to lay more stress on the pre-ideational than on the ideational factor in culture, that is to say, on the specific *pre*-conceptions or attitudes of life which underlie the different conceptions or ideals of life embodied in the conflicting cultures. The other is to interrelate historically these two factors within a determinate culture, thereby showing how its basic preconception of life arises as a general response on the part of the people of that culture to their particular environment, both physical and spiritual. The present chapter, which applies this thesis to the specific area of the two Americas, can serve as an illustration of the importance of the rôle of the pre-ideational factor in culture.

Philosophers are inveterate intellectualists by profession. They have been so accustomed to regarding the proper study of moral philosophy as having to do exclusively with the competing *conceptions* of the good life that they have tended to neglect the study of the distinct *preconceptions* peoples intuitively hold about life itself. Witness the impressive list of philosophers' philosophies from Thales on. Probably one reason for the one-sidedness in their subject-matter is that philosophers have been too provincial to take the trouble to analyze what happens to be obvious to our

14

particular society, thus conveniently forgetting or ignoring the fundamental issue of cultural relativity. Another and perhaps more plausible reason is the difficulty of the undertaking itself. After all, it takes a special effort to analyze such familiar things as the preconceptions we hold dear concerning ourselves and our destiny. Matters of faith, by definition, are harder to understand than matters of fact.

While the bulk of this book is concerned with the written philosophies of the most influential thinkers in contemporary Mexico, my purpose here is to say something about the unwritten philosophy of the Mexican people. And in the hope of making the underlying pattern of the Mexican mind more easily discernible, I am going to consider it from the larger perspective of the Latin-American mentality, of which it is a conspicuous representative, and compare it briefly with that of the United States.

To generalize about the peculiar mentality of a people or a group of peoples is, in reality, to formulate their particular philosophy of life. Of course, it goes without saying that any generalization about the collective character of either America incurs a logical risk, but there is no other alternative than to take the risk if we would understand. This is no denial of the responsibility to search for the most adequate interpretation of the national character of any people, nor is it a denial that the national characteristics themselves are subject to historical change and thus in continual need of empirical reinterpretation.

In this connection it would be in order to refer to an interesting paper by Charles Morris read at the Second East-West Philosophers' Conference (1949) in Honolulu, the title of which was "Comparative Strength of Life-Ideals in Eastern and Western Cultures." Its thesis is that a science of values on the intercultural level is possible only through a "quantitative study of the strength of the attitudes which underlie the life-ideals found in various cultures." If Professor Morris is right, then some day we shall be able to get direct evidence for or against our pet theories concerning the diverse ways of life among peoples. Meanwhile, however, we must rest content with opinions based partly on observation and partly on intuition. In any case, the writer pretends to do no more in what follows than preliminary spade work in a field most of us, doubtless with some justification, fear to tread.

To arrive at a people's philosophy it is necessary to determine their dominant preconception or peculiar *sense* of life. In other words, to interpret a people's character is to reveal what makes them "tick." To find out what makes a people "tick" we must try to uncover the mainspring of their history.

Everyone knows that the New World was discovered by an Italian (with apologies to the Norsemen) and colonized by the Portuguese, the Spanish, the French, the Dutch and the British. It was *not* colonized by the Russians (except for Alaska in the late 18th century) or the Japanese. This is, of course, stating what is historically obvious; yet it needs to be kept constantly in mind whenever we tell the fascinating story of America. As far as her post-Conquest heritage is concerned, America not only belongs to the Occident as opposed to the Orient; she belongs for the most part, to be exact, to the western as opposed to the eastern part of Europe. For it was precisely western Europe which originally bestowed upon her a common patrimony, whose norms can be formulated in the terse language of the late Frederick Woodbridge: "to think like Greeks, plunder like Romans and pray like Christians." [4] It is this common inheritance that has stamped the peoples of America with a peculiar status, that of *dependency* on European culture. Notwithstanding the gradual disappearance of their Mother Countries after the successive Wars of Independence beginning in the last quarter of the eighteenth century, their Mother Cultures still remain, to a significant extent, with us.

Well known also is the fact that the British colonists settled in New England in the seventeenth century and that the Spaniards settled in New Spain almost a hundred years before. Ever since then America has been split in two major parts, Anglo-America and Hispano-America (the latter term includes Brazil). As to the sources of their cultural divergences, Anglo-American culture descends from such movements as the English Reformation, European liberalism, modern science, British empiricism and the Industrial Revolution. On the other hand, Hispano-American culture, *in so far as it is European,* stems from the Hispanic Renaissance and Counter-Reformation, with all their ramifications. This leads to the crucial difference between the two cultures of America, to wit: Whereas Anglo-American culture is essentially European or, if we like, British through and through, Hispano-American culture is only partially European, having as it does an Indian (and, to a lesser degree, a Negro) cultural component. The Mexican philosopher José Vasconcelos has called our attention to the fact that "whenever two civilizations meet, one or the other becomes predominant, but they both undergo a change; they both lose certain traits and win others. What had happened to the Spaniard during the Arab invasion, happened to the Indian during the Spanish invasion." [5]

The above difference in cultural background is not only important in that it implies that the *Conquistadores* were, on the whole, more humane in their treatment of the Indians than their English counterpart. The difference is important for a more telling reason. For while the culture of Anglo-America is relatively *pure* in the sense that it is at bottom generically European and specifically British, the culture of Hispano-America, on the contrary, is essentially *hybrid* in that its European parts are mixed with Indian and Negro cultural elements. Not to mention the mixture of climates throughout Latin America, more significant than the biological fact that some Latin Americans are *mestizo* in blood is that all of them are *mestizo* in culture.

The cultural *mestizaje* of Latin America is a fact generally recognized by present-day authorities from both sides of the Rio Grande. It is, however, in the interpretation of this fundamental fact that they are divided. Paradoxically enough, those above the border tend to be optimistic about the cultural hybridism of their neighbors to the south; those below are inclined to be pessimistic. Of the two groups, the latter is probably closer to the truth. To be concrete, it is sufficient to mention in passing the research work done by Samuel Ramos and Leopoldo Zea of Mexico, both of whom have shown how the "inferiority complex" of the Mexican people is related to their *mestizo* type of culture. Details are to be found in the final chapter and in *Aspects of Mexican Civilization* (1926) by José Vasconcelos and Manuel Gamio. On the other side, Waldo Frank and Filmer Northrop have come to the opposite conclusion. The first, who is quick to perceive that "the mestizo, born of the marriage of Spain and Amerindia," is the "perfect symbol for the inward complexity of all Hispano-Americans," spoils his insight by failing to emphasize that the child itself of that married couple has tended all along to feel torn between the distinct values of its parents. Moreover, he destroys the very "inward complexity" of the *mestizo* soul on the next page of his article, "The Hispano-American's World," published in *The Nation* (1941), by declaring that Catholic culture "harmonizes with the intuitive values" of the pre-Conquest Indian cultures, with their "pantheism and aesthetic genius." [6] But, if there had been in Latin America as much harmonization of European and Indian values as the author claims, how could one ever come to terms with Leopoldo Zea's obvious statement that the typical Latin American has felt like an "illegitimate child" of Europe?

Similarly, Professor Northrop sees more harmony of parts in the so-called "rich culture" of Mexico than even her own national-minded investigators are willing to admit. Employing a distinction in the field of chemistry, he concocts with his four components of Mexican culture—the Indian, the Spanish colonial, the French influence in the nineteenth century, and contemporary humanism —too much of a neat compound out of what is still a rather disconcerting mixture of parts. A hybrid or *mestizo* culture, by hypothesis, can't be quite so well adjusted to things as Northrop imagines. In all fairness, however, it should be noted that his book, *The Logic of the Sciences and the Humanities* (1947), shows more sensitivity to the "cultural conflicts" within contemporary Mexican society than is to be found in his account of Mexican culture in *The Meeting of East and West* (1946), where his sympathies as an Indianist lead him to make too much of the Virgin of Guadalupe.[7]

After differentiating the two basic patterns of culture that prevail in America in the light of their historical origins, next it is necessary to try to remove one or two popular misconceptions about them.

About ten years ago Aldous Huxley took a hurried trip to Mexico City, after which he declared in a local magazine that Mexican culture is not made of the "Fords and Frigidaires" north of the border, but "continues to be, pre-eminently French."[8] Now, no matter how good Mr. Huxley may be as a novelist, he is not so good as an observer of the two cultures in question, notwithstanding the apparent truth of his clever remark. For, in the first place, he commits the usual error of the foreigner and, alas, of some of our own countrymen, in narrowing the vision of North America to what, say, the city of Detroit symbolizes. And in the second place, he commits the worse error (due probably to his jibe as an Englishman at the grandeur that was Spain) of not realizing that the culture of Mexico is obviously Mexican, and, furthermore, that of all the European cultures entering into her complex make-up, it is *Spain,* not France, which during the last four centuries has made the most continuous contribution towards what she is in language, religion, customs, social institutions, and ideology. After all, colonial Mexico was New Spain, *not* New France, for three hundred years. That length of time cannot be dismissed cavalierly or explained away by conspicuous silence. Without denying the important influence of France on Mexico, especially throughout the last century, the historical fact, nonetheless, is that the latter's culture, as far as her European elements are concerned, has remained Spanish, not French, ever since that Brave New World of Fernando Cortéz came into being at the dawn of the sixteenth century.

Incidentally, it is not only Aldous Huxley who claims that Mexican culture continues to be pre-eminently French. Strange as it may sound, most Latin-American observers have been urging the same view until quite recently, not only with respect to Mexico but also with respect to Latin America as a whole. For instance, Francisco García Calderón, a distinguished writer of Peru, in a paper presented in Heidelberg at the Third International Congress of Philosophy (1908) on "Philosophical Currents in Latin America," stated flatly that her post-Independence thought is of "French origin." [9] But the Peruvian *literato* missed the forest for the trees. For the truth of the matter is that whatever ideas are imported into, say, Mexico, undergo a process of acculturation, the assimilative phase of which may be called, in this particular case, "Hispanization," while the other, the adaptive, may be called "Mexicanization." In short, Mexicans don't take imported ideas, as they do their pulque, straight. *Mutatis mutandis,* the same two phases operate in the rest of America, whether the original Mother Cultures be French, British, Portuguese or Spanish. An excellent illustration of how philosophical importations get "hispanized" and "mexicanized" is to be found in the Franco-British positivistic movement in Mexico, treated in the next chapter.

In regard to our own country, it is not only those judging us from a European distance who contend that we worship at the feet of God the Machine. People closer to us and, as a matter of fact, even at home make the same hasty pronouncement. For example, Waldo Frank laments over "the jungle of the machine" that overwhelms us and complains of our "shallow vision of life." Of course, practically all Latin-American intellectuals, who doubtless have more reason to dislike the so-called American Way of Life than our own Waldo Frank, bring the same old charge against us. One of the most prominent of these is the late Mexican painter José Clemente Orozco. According to his authoritative interpreter, Justino Fernández, Orozco sees us as a gregarious yet lonely people, a people full of "scientific superstition and impiety." [10] This judgment on the part of the great Mexican muralist is unfortunate, but what makes it more so is that Professor Northrop of Yale presumably sympathizes with it. Although he discusses the culture of the United States as a "vision of freedom" in his chief work to date, at the same time he shows sympathy with that fresco of Orozco's at Dartmouth College (*Anglo-America*), which pictures us as a people with "pollyannic ideals." Some phenomena in our society do reflect a pollyannic tendency, but is it fair to give the impression that this is our ideal? Our ideal, after all, is made in the image of Daniel Boone, not George Babbitt! It is, in a word, Whitmanesque.

All the foregoing considerations can now be brought into focus. The key proposition of this chapter is as follows: the dominant preconception on which Hispano-American culture rests is the *tragic* sense of life and, in contrast, that on which Anglo-American culture rests is the *epic* sense of life. What is the connection between the tragic sense of life and the relatively *hetero-*

geneous culture of Latin America, and the connection between the epic sense of life and the relatively *homogeneous* culture of the United States? Since the dominant preconceptions of the two Americas have been distinguished in aesthetic terms, an adequate answer to our question presupposes, as even Croce would have to admit, an empirical distinction at least between the tragic and the epic.

The theme common to the tragic and the epic forms of literature is a dramatic situation involving the inevitability of moral conflict arising out of the pursuit of some goal by a personality or a group. As to their difference in content and context, briefly stated it is this: while the epic soul struggles endlessly to conquer obstacles external to himself, the tragic soul has the more difficult job of conquering himself. The substance of the tragic is not, as the traditional theory of tragedy maintains, the conflict between good and evil. Such is, in fact, the polarity of the epic situation. For the epic hero looks upon the very obstacles he encounters in his ventures as *evil* to be overcome. The stuff that all strictly tragic situations are made of is, rather, the subtler *conflict between goods,* as the greatest tragedies of the world make manifest. So much so that we may say: whereas the epic represents the problem of evil in art, the tragic represents the problem of good. As in art, so in life.

What is, historically, the relation between the tragic attitude the peoples of Latin America have towards life and their relatively *heterogeneous* pattern of culture? As the hero in a tragic drama is torn between conflicting goods, so the typical Latin American is torn between the values and ideals of his pre-Conquest Indian heritage on the one side, and those of his European heritage on the other. It is precisely at the crossroads of these two inheritances that the roots of Latin-American culture converge and diverge. The tragic sense of life is what pervades the resulting dilemma, the dual character manifest in the *mestizo* temper of all its institutions. In short, to behold the Latin-American scene is to behold a veritable Hispano-Indian Tragedy on a large scale, to which we respond with both pity and admiration (*not* "pity and fear," Aristotle notwithstanding).

To ascertain the historical connection between the epic sense of life and our relatively *homogeneous* pattern of culture, it is necessary to resume a point already touched on a few pages back. The difference in treatment the American Indians received at the hands of their Latin and British conquerors is a prime factor which must be taken into serious consideration in differentiating the two primary cultures of America. For one thing, the Spaniards did not execute to the bitter end the once popular dictum that "the only good Indian is a dead Indian"; for another, they were not so fussy about intermarrying with the natives. On the other hand, once our own forefathers no longer had to worry about the Red Men, the epic or pioneer spirit could be developed to their heart's content without many pangs of conscience. At any rate, this is precisely the case with the grand old story of the American Frontier, which one of our American historians at Columbia University in a recent New York *Times* review of a book on the subject describes as the "epic sweep of the westward movement." [11] In the same issue there appears also a review of a book called *The Epic of American Industry*.

The appearance of these two reviews within the covers of one of our most widely-read magazines seems to be definitely symptomatic of the Anglo-American climate of culture. Everybody knows that it is the ambition of the historical novelist in the United States to write *the* American Epic. And when even as prosaic a thing as our business world gets its latest *Apologia* for free enterprise glorified in poetic terms, *The Epic of American Industry,* we can infer with some confidence that we are not dealing with only a pretty metaphor. Needless to say, our Puritan and democratic traditions are, of course, the religious and political expressions, respectively, of our epic sense of life. What the late President Franklin D. Roosevelt declared at a critical moment of world affairs, namely, that our generation had a "rendezvous with Destiny," applies to all generations of North Americans, inasmuch as his felicitous phrase suits perfectly a people like ours, ever confident of achieving bigger and better things, material and spiritual. And were we to compare the other America's mentality with ours, the corresponding phrase which comes closest to revealing her tragic sense of life would be that of the Mexico-inspired American poet Alan Seeger: "rendezvous with Death."

Nowhere perhaps does the difference between the American and the Mexican character come out more clearly into the open than in the field of sports, and especially at a bullfight. From time to time we hear of incidents at a bullfight where Mexicans become enraged when Americans cheer for the bull. This happens because Mexicans, like Spaniards, take their bullfights seriously. It is not just a game to them, as baseball is to us, but a graceful ritual symbolizing the tragic sense of life, with all its forebodings. So serious is the ritual to them that on Sundays their custom is to go to church in the morning to commemorate Life and to the bullfight in the afternoon to commemorate Death. Ernest Hemingway has caught its significance in *Death in the Afternoon.* In fact, the Mexican historian Edmundo O'Gorman has gone so far as to suggest at the end of his recent book, *Crisis y porvenir de la ciencia histórica,* a theory of human existence which takes its point of departure from the experience at a bullfight.

The point has been reached for a brief consideration of how the distinct mentality of the two Americas is reflected in their philosophical activity. Such a consideration leads to a possible correlation between a philosopher's philosophy and his people's philosophy.

It is commonly recognized that the characteristic philosophy of the United States is Pragmatism. This is admitted (doubtless with regret) even by anti-pragmatists. But still the fact itself requires some explanation. To understand it, the following hypothesis is helpful: pragmatism as a philosophy and the epic sense of life go together. For pragmatism is, in essence, the philosophy of human *achievement*. In other words, it is the theoretical expression of the epic sense of life. As an epic celebrates the life of achievement in action, so pragmatism defends the same way of life in theory. Pioneers are pragmatists by instinct. Witness our folk heroes, such as Paul Bunyan and Mike Fink, and compare them with Periquillo Sarniento, their Mexican counterpart. If this is correct, it is no longer an academic mystery that William James and John Dewey are so highly respected among us. After all, they are our *vox populi* on the philosophical plane.

What philosophy, it might be asked, is the unique expression of the Latin-American sense of life? This question is harder to answer simply because philosophical thought in Latin America has not as yet reached the point of development already visible in the pragmatic movement of the United States, though there are many signs at present that that philosophy is on its way. In the meantime, unless we are mistaken in reading the current signs, the germs of that nascent philosophy look like some theistic species of existentialism—to resort to an overworked term these days—"theistic" because Latin America is steeped in Roman Catholic traditions and "existentialism" because this is the philosophy of human *failure* in the ultimate and deepest signification. In short, existentialism is to the tragic sense of life what pragmatism is to the epic sense.

The cultures of the two Americas having been traced very

briefly back to their psychological origins, at this point some proof is needed for the conclusions reached in our psychogenetic comparison. Unfortunately, given the present state of intercultural knowledge, there is only indirect evidence at the moment. On the philosophical side of the question, at least, this much may be said, namely, that a difference of emphasis exists between our own way of thinking and that of our neighbors to the south. The general orientation of our inquiries is, in the main, towards problems of fact; this is evident from our ever-growing interest in modern science and technology. A scientific philosophy, after all, is the natural expression of a people with an epic sense of life. Probably the most crucial episodes in the American Epic have been and are still being wrought in our laboratories, the quiet yet key places dedicated to the conquest and control of Nature by means of human intelligence.

Whereas North American thought has been largely motivated by an interest in the problems of knowledge, Latin-American thought has been inspired essentially by problems of conduct. The latter's concern over normative issues reflects a tragic sense of life. Since the preconception concerning the tragic character of life is born out of man's moral struggle with himself and the society in which he lives, its conceptual expression should correspond in content. With a few exceptions perhaps, this is precisely what happens in the story of philosophy in the countries of Latin America. So much so that Francisco García Calderón in his Heidelberg paper came to the conclusion that the philosophical ideas which have endured in Latin America have been essentially social in kind. The same point has been recently developed with many illustrations by José Gaos, a Spanish refugee residing at present in Mexico City. Gaos not only shows that the characteristic themes of Hispano-American thought since the Enlightenment have centered around problems of conduct, but also indicates the remarkable affinity between the content of these themes and their form of expression. The typical *pensador* below the Rio Grande, like the French *philosophe* of the eighteenth century, writes popular essays on morals and politics rather than technical treatises on logic and metaphysics, and speaks in the public square or café more than he writes. In a word, his thought is "non-systematic." [12] A typical title is *Discursos a la nación mexicana* by the late Antonio Caso of Mexico. The English reader, incidentally, can get the same general impression of what and how Latin Americans think from *A Century of Latin-American Thought* (1944) by William Rex Crawford, the first secondary source book on the market dealing Laertius-like with the lives and opinions of some thirty-five "patriot-thinkers" from Latin America during the last hundred years.

Finally, to sum up, the secret imaginative background of the philosophizing characteristic of America is, on the one hand, the tragic sense of life rooted in Latin-American existentialism and, on the other, the epic sense of life rooted in Anglo-American pragmatism. However distinct these two philosophies of the good life may be, I should venture to say that a synthesis or meeting of North and South America is possible on the ground that they complement each other and share a common faith, namely, a humanistic attitude towards life, together with an heroic conception of man. Such is, at any rate, my vision of the two Americas, a Brave New World big enough and free enough to leave room for two kinds of human heroes, epic and tragic.

2

**Five Stages
in Mexican Thought**

The development of the Mexican mind since colonial days, viewed philosophically, may be analyzed into five principal stages: (1) the Scholastic, (2) the Enlightenment, (3) the Anti-Rationalistic, (4) the Positivistic, (5) the Anti-Positivistic. As the aim of this book is to connect philosophical ideas with social circumstances and aspirations in Mexico, it is necessary to discuss those ideas in relation with the general history of that country, rather than in isolation. For our purposes, therefore, we may divide the social history of Mexico into five respective periods. To employ the mnemonic device of 4 R's and one counter-R, these are: (1) the Counter-Reformation, (2) the Revolt, (3) the Reform, (4) the Reconstruction, (5) the Revolution.

Two diametrically opposed kinds of reductionist fallacy are to be avoided in writing the sort of historical survey proposed. One is the practical man's mistake; the other is the theoretical man's. The most common case of the first is the economic determinism of the traditional Marxist, who tries to explain human history by reducing it to economic terms. A current example of the second is Northrop's ideological determinism, which claims that the "presuppositions of a culture determine its empirical manifestations and institutions." To quote at length the illustrations from Mexican culture he gives on the same page:[1]

> Certainly the predominantly Catholic society of colonial Mexico, with its baroque architecture, its hierarchical, monarchical political order, and its widely extended, deeply moving, religious sentiments, is not to be understood apart from the basic beliefs of medieval Spanish Roman Catholicism. It is clear, also beyond doubt in this instance, that the beliefs of Aristotle, Saint Thomas and Las Casas came first and that the facts and institutions of colonial Mexico came afterwards. It is equally clear in the Mexican culture of the nineteenth century that the philosophical ideas of Voltaire and the French Encyclopaedists preceded the democratic, political revolution of 1810 and the subsequent nationalization of church property and secularization of education. In similar fashion, the social philosophy of Comte preceded and defined the pattern which determined social and political policy in Mexico between 1876 and 1910 under the dictatorship of Porfirio Diaz. Likewise, the philosophy of Marx, as conveyed to the Mexican intelligentsia and the masses by the paintings of Diego Rivera and David Alfaro Siqueiros, preceded by means of their influence during the 1920's and early 1930's the six-year plan of the Cardenas regime during the years from 1934 to 1940.

The above quotation is almost a perfect instance of the fallacious assumption that whatever precedes an event is therefore its cause or, putting the same thing in the usual form of the fallacy found in a logic text, that whatever follows an event is therefore caused by it (*post hoc ergo propter hoc*). Besides, the irony of the ideological interpretation of human history under consideration is that its author accuses an idealist like Hegel and a materialist like Marx of committing "the culturalistic fallacy" in their identification of the normative "ought" with the historical "is." Yet, at the same time, Northrop himself commits that very fallacy in a more radical manner inasmuch as he vigorously contends that ideas, which are matters of culture, are the causal agents of the tides of history. Thus he succeeds, to put it in Biblical language, in pulling the mote out of their eye but, alas, fails to cast out the beam from his own. As to the value of Northrop's accent on the ideological factors in the story of civilization, it is doubtless a much needed corrective to the materialistic interpretation of history. But, like most reactions, it runs to the other extreme. The man who sees the defects of both sides of the argument is Bertrand Russell:[2]

> Two opposite errors, both common, are to be guarded against. On the one hand, men who are more familiar with books than with affairs are apt to overestimate the influence of philosophers. When they see some political party proclaiming itself inspired by So-and-So's teaching, they think its actions are attributable to So-and-So, whereas, not infrequently, the philosopher is only acclaimed because he recommended what the party would have done in any case. Writers of books, until recently, almost all exaggerated the effects of their predecessors in the same trade. But conversely, a new error has arisen by reaction against the old one, and this new error consists in regarding theorists as almost passive products of their circumstances, and as having hardly any influence at all upon the course of events. Ideas, according to this view, are the froth on the surface of deep currents, which are determined by material and technical causes: social changes are no more caused by thought than the flow of a river is caused by the bubbles that reveal its direction to an onlooker. For my part, I believe that the truth lies between these two extremes. Between ideas and practical life, as everywhere else, there is reciprocal interaction; to ask which is cause and which effect is as futile as the problem of the hen and the egg.

There is one more preliminary matter of importance which must be settled before giving a brief sketch of the five stages in

Mexican thought. Though the previous chapter emphasized that the New World is, by and large, a cultural dependent of western Europe, at the same time the implication was that the intellectual importations assimilated have undergone a phase of adaptation. Consequently, when the Argentine scholar Risieri Frondizi categorically denies originality to Latin-American philosophy on the ground of its being merely a "restatement" [3] of European philosophical problems, he seems to be making an understatement. True, European culture has supplied Latin-Americans with the tools for the solution of their problems, but it is equally true that the tools themselves have had to be somewhat transformed in order to suit new historical conditions. Even Herbert W. Schneider, who does not flatter our own national ego when he declares that North Americans "still live intellectually on the fringe of European culture," is careful to add immediately that the intellectual goods we import from Europe "are not being swallowed raw; they must be blended with those home-grown ideas, for which an established taste and preference exists." [4] These two phases of acculturation—assimilation *ab extra* and adaptation *ab intra*—implicit in Professor Schneider's statement, are evident, to a greater or lesser degree, in the entire intellectual history of all the peoples of America. Accordingly, whatever originality Latin-American philosophy can boast of lies precisely in those particular ways it has reacted to its inherited Mother Philosophies. This book can serve to substantiate the point just made, inasmuch as philosophy in Latin America is essentially philosophy in Mexico writ large.

I. THE SCHOLASTIC STAGE

Since the Scholastic stage in Mexican thought recalls the old story of the direct transfer of Spain's Counter-Reformation to the New World, we need not say much about it. Therewith, New Spain inherited the orthodox doctrines promulgated at the Council

of Trent, the Jesuit Society, and all the paraphernalia of the Inquisition. Philosophy in colonial Mexico played the same rôle,
of course, as she did in the Middle Ages: handmaiden to the
Roman Catholic Church. Philosophical activity was confined
mostly to *quaestiones disputatae* in theology and, of the various
scholastic traditions involved in settling such disputes, the Thomist
—especially its Suárez version—was the one that finally won out.
Aristotle expurgated was the authority of the natural world; St.
Thomas, of the supernatural. Church and Crown ruled together
ad maiorem Dei gloriam for three centuries.

However, the history of Scholasticism in Mexico during the
colonial period is not just a simple orthodox affair. To begin with,
the *Physica Speculatio* (Mexico City, 1557), which was written by
the first philosopher in America and "the father of Mexican
philosophy," Fray Alonso de la Vera Cruz, not only reveals the
original vigor of Spanish Scholasticism, but also anticipates the
subsequent interest in modern science on the part of the Schoolmen during the colonial period. We learn, moreover, that around
the middle of the sixteenth century the Renaissance humanism of
Erasmus entered secretly into New Spain via its first bishop, Fray
Juan de Zumárraga.[5] About the same time, in 1537, Fray Bartolomé de las Casas, the great Spanish apologist for the American
Indian, wrote *De unico vocationis modo omnium gentium ad
Veram Religionem*. Its thesis is that there is only one way decreed
by God for teaching men the true religion, namely, "the one which
convinces the understanding in a rational manner and satisfies
the will." This way is "common to all men of the world, regardless of errors, sects, or vices."[6] Imagine an anti-authoritarian statement like that coming from an evangelizing Thomist in the
sixteenth century! According to Edmundo O'Gorman, Las Casas'
treatise, however ambiguous its philosophical position, is of interest because it reflects in its very ambiguity a period of transition

between the medieval and modern climates of opinion, a "link" between St. Thomas and Descartes.[7]

In the second half of the eighteenth century several attempts were made to reform Scholasticism by injecting into it new winds of doctrine from overseas. To illustrate, mention may be made of the efforts of Andrés de Guevara and of Juan Benito Díaz de Gamarra to revamp Scholastic thought along scientific lines. Guevara, a Jesuit whose mind was tinged with Newtonian and Gassendian ideas, went so far as to charge that the language of Scholastic philosophy was "barbarous, uncivilized and horrible, its questions useless and vain, its power tyrannical and unbearable." [8] Gamarra, an Oratorian, preached eclecticism as a philosophy and proclaimed: "Fortunate are the eclectic philosophers, who imitating the bees seek from flower to flower the sweet nectar of science." [9] Having been inspired by Descartes, he attempted to temper Scholastic dogmatism with Cartesian rationalism. By questioning the principle of authority and appealing to the court of reason, these two priests prepared the ground for the subsequent infiltration of the Enlightenment spirit into New Spain, thus serving as the ideological precursors of the struggle for national independence. But how did modern thought manage to get through the colonial Office of Inquisition without suffering the usual fate?

In 1767 the Jesuit Society, which had virtual control of colonial education, was banned from the New World by order of Charles III. Along with the order of this "enlightened despot" came, for the first time in colonial history, permission for the free entry of books from overseas. The expulsion of the Jesuits and the introduction of new ideas, especially from France via Spain, not only were definite signs that the Church was losing her power, but, ironically enough, they also were an indication that the Crown was on the verge of losing it also. In short, Charles III's order turned out to be the Spanish Empire's Swan Song. The tocsin was actually sounded in New Spain in the middle of September of 1810, when one of her rural priests (Miguel Hidalgo) rallied "the cry of Dolores" against the Mother Country and became the Father of Mexican Independence. The knell of a parting empire had tolled.

II. THE ENLIGHTENMENT STAGE

There is a strong tradition in intellectual history which asserts that the Wars of Independence in the Spanish colonies sprang from the teachings of the French Enlightenment in the eighteenth century. Doubtless the planned attacks of the crusading *Philosophes* on superstition and ignorance as well as their *Culte de la Raison* were the last straw that broke the camel's back (the camel here being the Genteel Tradition of Scholasticism). Nevertheless, as the historian John Tate Lanning is quick to observe:[10]

> It has long been the custom of specialists to assume that the theoretical foundation of the revolt against Spain rested solely upon the ideas of the French political doctrinaires of 1789. A man dropping from Mars to investigate that subject, with all second-hand treatises destroyed and forced to use original papers exclusively, would perhaps not regard the names of Rousseau, Voltaire, Montesquieu, or even Raynal as significant enough to emphasize in the book which his association with earthly university professors would force him to write. No doubt these last gave the late colonial period a definite slant, but the names which would seem of transcendant importance in this hypothetical book would be instead, St. Thomas Aquinas, Descartes, Newton, Condillac, Pierre Gassendi, and Malebranche. Without them Raynal, Condorcet, Diderot, Benjamin Franklin, and Thomas Paine would scarcely have been heard and certainly not understood. An intellectual revolution in America involving these men was the only one consistent with the role of the church in the national period.

Although Lanning's thesis is a considerable improvement over the traditional explanation, which exaggerates the influence of the French Encyclopaedists on the political independence of the Spanish colonies in America, still the thesis itself seems to presuppose too much of a difference in temper between the two groups of thinkers listed—an assumption which is questionable. Carl Becker for one would question it as follows:[11]

> We are accustomed to think of the eighteenth century as essentially modern in its temper. Certainly, the *Philosophes* themselves made a great point of having renounced the superstition and hocus-pocus of medieval Christian thought, and we have usually been willing to take them at their word. Surely, we say, the eighteenth century was preeminently the age of reason, surely the *Philosophes* were a skeptical lot, atheists in effect if not by profession, addicted to science and the scientific method, always out to crush the infamous, valiant defenders of liberty, equality, fraternity, freedom of speech, and what you will. All very true. And yet I think the *Philosophes* were nearer the Middle Ages, less emancipated from the preconceptions of medieval Christian thought, than they quite realized or we have commonly supposed.

Whichever position is taken—Lanning's or Becker's—restoring as it does the continuity between the old rationalism and the new in the transition from the Scholastic to the Enlightenment stage of Mexican thought, helps us to understand what otherwise would be a mystery, namely, that a Catholic priest, of all people, should be the father of a country. Miguel Hidalgo was essentially an eclectic mind. He was a liberal in politics but a conservative in theology. As a follower of the Jesuit tradition of Francisco Suárez, the late sixteenth-century Spanish reformer of Thomas Aquinas, Hidalgo had been brought up on the democratic notion of popular sovereignty and hence was against political absolutism. Records[12] show that as a token of his faith in political liberalism, Hidalgo became a member of a Masonic Lodge in Mexico City in

1806, and as a protest against Napoleon's invasion of Spain in 1809, he joined a patriotic society in his parish town of Dolores. On the other hand, despite the recent claim of a young Mexican scholar that the Captain General of the Revolt against Spain initiated a "theological revolution"[13] in his *Disertación sobre el verdadero método de estudiar Teología Escolástica* (1784), Samuel Ramos is probably right when he reminds us that Hidalgo was too much of a Jesuit in mentality to be revolutionary in theology.[14]

It would certainly be the height of historical naïveté to think that the so-called *grito de Dolores* instigated by a captain-priest came out of the blue to start all the trouble in New Spain. Battle-cries are the pretexts of history, not its texts. Mexican historians with a conservative or Catholic viewpoint, like Lucas Alamán and Antonio Gibaja y Patrón, have gone out of their way to show the tremendous impact of Freemasonry and the foreign interests of France, England and the United States upon the insurrection of New Spain. But this putting the blame on the outsider is an old trick. For the probable truth of the matter, as a present-day Spaniard himself sees it, is that the independence of the Spanish colonies in America was won at the expense of the decadence of the Mother Country. According to José Gaos,[15] it was precisely in the eighteenth century when Spain was in her full grandeur that her decadence and the idea of decadence were simultaneously born. As soon as the secularizing attitude of the Enlightenment infiltrated into Spain, she became conscious of her decadence, and her thinkers, led by Father Benito Jerónimo Feijóo, came to realize that her decadence was due to her having championed the Counter-Reformation in the preceding two centuries. To remedy the sad state of affairs, they urged Spain to put away childish things and become up-to-date. Unfortunately, however, their appeal to modernity arrived not only too late to save her, but too late to save her colonies in the next century. The idea of decadence in the metropolis begot with time the idea of independence in the colonies, and everybody knows that the latter would not hold its peace until it became a political reality like its predecessors, the American and French Revolutions.

Evidence for the compromising ideology of the Mexican Revolt against Spain can be garnered from the documents[16] on the War of Independence. These documents contain three chief items: (1) the Declaration of Independence itself, (2) Roman Catholicism as the State religion, and (3) the protection of private property. To satisfy the Marxist interpreters of history, who see the economic motive all over the map of human affairs, it should be added that part of Hidalgo's program in 1810 was to get the land back to the Indians. Of course, this did not materialize and the Indians were not taken into account until a hundred years later. At all events, the three provisions stipulated by the War documents were incorporated into the first major Constitution of Mexico in 1824. The next Constitution of 1857 radically changed the religious provision by separating Church and State; the last one of 1917 theoretically got rid of the economic provision in its Article 27, defining property as an exclusive right of the State. Therefore, of the three original provisions which take us back to Mexico's transition period between colonial status and nationhood, only the first one, national sovereignty, has been left intact, legally speaking. Nonetheless, we should remember that in Mexico, as elsewhere, there is a gap between what a Constitution says on paper and what is done in fact.

To return to the intellectual side of the Revolt, Father Hidalgo carried on his campaign for self-government under the eclectic banner of Catholic liberalism. He fought with the Sword of Freedom in his right hand and with the Virgin of Guadalupe in his left. Either he saw no incompatibility in the work of the two hands or he applied the Biblical counsel concerning alms to arms:

"let not thy left hand know what thy right hand doeth." Yet, having separated in typical Jesuit fashion his liberal faith in politics from his conservative faith in religion, there is one thing he did not and could hardly foresee, namely, that what started as a movement of emancipation from the Mother Country was destined to become a movement of emancipation from the Mother Church. In any case, Hidalgo's voice of protest against his Crown was transformed shortly afterwards by others less compromising into a boomerang against his Church. The half-revolution he had started turned out to be an unexpected invitation for the opponents of the Church to finish the other half. This is precisely what took place when the anti-Catholic liberals joined forces. The colonial Office of Inquisition, smelling the rat (Hidalgo's nickname, by the way, was "the Fox") and being shrewd enough to recognize that Catholic liberalism would sooner or later beget its illegitimate variety, tried to stop the "cry" of one of its members who yelled out of turn by hurling at him the old accusation of heresy. But it was too late. The spark had already been put to the combustible pile of general discontent in the Spanish colonial world and no anathema could artificially extinguish it. The protestant seed had been sown unwittingly by an obscure Catholic priest and the Mexican Reform came to reap its anti-clerical fruits in the Constitution of 1857. At last the Enlightenment had arrived in full swing in Mexico, and woe unto any one who did not see the new light!

III. THE ANTI-RATIONALISTIC STAGE

The theme that dominates nineteenth-century thought in Mexico, as elsewhere in Latin America, is the European-born idea of liberalism. But, needless to insist nowadays, liberalism is a "weasel" word whose definition can only be guessed from the context in which it is used. At least three distinct meanings emerge from the Mexican discussions on that subject of political and social theory during the nineteenth century. These are in historical order: (1) the rationalistic, (2) the anti-rationalistic and (3) the positivistic conception of freedom. It is the second meaning which interests us at the moment.

The anti-rationalistic view of liberalism constitutes the common faith of the spokesmen for that hectic period in Mexican history called *la Reforma*. The Reform is the epoch immediately following the War of Independence, covering roughly the second third of the last century. The chief preoccupation of the Reform Generation was to extend the area of independence from the sphere of politics to that of culture. They wanted, in a word, to emancipate the Mexican mind. Emancipate it from what? First of all, emancipate it in practice from the colonial mentality, which, despite the winning of political independence, continued to rule and ruin Mexico in sundry ways; secondly, emancipate it in theory from the Enlightenment variety of liberalism, which was accused of being utopian and abstract. With the birth of a new nation on their hands, the Mexican Reformers naturally went about trying to uproot colonial manners and morals left and right. They tried hard but failed to be effective until 1857 or thereabouts. For one thing, General Antonio López de Santa Anna proved too much for them. Might made right! Mexico, although national in letter, remained at bottom colonial in spirit.

When we turn from the negative to the positive side of the emancipation proclamation at the time of the Reform, we find that the *grupo progresista* sought to modernize the Mexican mind by preaching a less formalist or more historicist type of liberalism, that is, a type relevant to *Mexican* circumstances. Their anti-rationalistic conception of freedom was, of course, a manifestation of the romantic and nationalistic reaction in the early part of the nineteenth century against the cosmopolitanism of the Natural Rights doctrine characteristic of the so-called Age of Reason. The anti-rationalistic note is evinced by the philosophical currents popular then in Mexico, which included Destutt de Tracy's *Idéologie,* Victor Cousin's eclecticism, German historicism, French traditionalism and British utilitarianism.[17]

The intellectual leader of the "progressive group" was a Mexican historian by the name of José María Luis Mora, author of the Reform Plan of 1833. The sources of his social philosophy included Benjamin Constant, Pierre Cabanis, Destutt de Tracy, Montesquieu, Jeremy Bentham and James Mill. Of all these influences, British utilitarianism had the greatest effect upon his political and economic liberalism. Mora's opinion concerning the outcome of the Mexican Revolt against Spain was far from optimistic. All it had really accomplished was to free his people of foreign masters only to have them fall prey to native ones, the army and the clergy. Consequently, he urged the separation of economic and political power so that Mexicans would no longer have to depend for their means of subsistence on whatever *cacique* happened to be in the government saddle. After all, he illustrated, the middle classes of England and the United States had managed to be quite successful in carrying out the experiment of keeping the two kinds of power separate. And it was his hope that Mexican society would reform itself gradually along the same lines through "mental revolutions," not armed ones. Finally, he urged Mexicans to discard the myth that a form of government is a "magic formula" for bringing prosperity and thus to come to the realization that:[18]

> Work, industry, and wealth make a man really and reliably virtuous. In rendering him independent of all the rest, these three imbue him with the firmness and noble valor of character which resist oppression and baffle any attempt at bribery. He who has never had to toady to power and to beg from it his means of subsistence is certain not to

support power in its devious ways, its schemes of disorganization, its tyranny.

Mora's apologetic for the virtues of the forthcoming middle class in Mexico anticipates the ideology of Mexican positivism.

IV. THE POSITIVISTIC STAGE

The anti-clerical and anti-rationalistic campaign of the Mexican liberals during the Reform period helped to prepare the ground for the introduction of positivism into Mexico. A bibliographical note is appropriate at this point. The rise and fall of Mexican positivism, covering roughly the period from 1867 to 1910, has been made the subject of an exhaustive study by Leopoldo Zea of Mexico. He published two volumes some years ago on the topic and, fortunately for the English reader, a resumé of his findings now appears in an article called "Positivism and Porfirism in Latin America," which, in spite of its broad title, deals mostly with the positivistic movement in Mexico. His whole approach amounts to an application of Karl Mannheim's general idea—every ideology is an instrument of a determinate class in society—to the Mexican situation under positivism. The author's thesis[19] is briefly this: positivism in Mexico was the ideological expression of the Mexican bourgeoisie. Mora was the "first theorist" of the middle class in Mexico. This middle class, however, should not be confused with its European counterpart. For notwithstanding its aspirations to become industrialist, the Mexican middle class was composed of big landowners, who instead of exploiting the resources of industry exploited the peasants and the national treasury. Moreover, as to the actual industries developed in Mexico during the nineteenth century, these had their source in foreign interests, French and English in particular, to which the *burguesía mexicana* played the rôle of handmaiden.

What follows leans rather heavily on Zea's research work in the field. And in spite of the assumption for the present purposes that his scholarship is essentially sound, still it is only fair to say beforehand that he does not tell his prolix story of Mexican positivism from a positivistic point of view. His own philosophical standpoint is discussed in the last chapter.

According to this Mexican scholar, the positivistic movement in Mexico exhibits two successive phases: the first is the combative and the other, the constructive. Each of these phases, as we are about to see, reflects different circumstances in Mexican history. The man who lived through both of them is the importer of Auguste Comte's philosophy into Mexico, Gabino Barreda. While Barreda was studying medicine in Paris, he was introduced to the French philosopher by Pedro Contreras Elizalde, "the first Mexican positivist." [20] Barreda attended Comte's lectures at the Palais Royal from 1849 to 1851 and became a convert to the *Catéchisme Positiviste*. On completing his medical studies in the latter year, he returned to his native land and joined the Liberal Party.

The first public notice of Barreda the positivist comes from his "Civic Oration" delivered in the town of Guanajuato on the sixteenth of September, 1867, in commemoration of Independence Day. Adapting Comte's system to the Mexican situation as he saw it then, Barreda advances a positivistic interpretation of Mexican history, dividing it into the three well-known stages of social evolution: (1) the theological, (2) the metaphysical and (3) the positive. The first he takes to be represented by the colonial period, the second by the Revolt, the last by the Reform. This address justifies the ways of the Liberal Party to Mexicans. Its main accent is on the glorious contributions of anti-rationalistic liberalism towards emancipating the Mexican mind from its theological shackles and metaphysical abstractions. Since the address itself identifies liberalism with the positivistic stage of politics, it illustrates the initial or combative phase of Mexican positivism, joining hands with the radical liberals against the common enemy, the clergy and the army. But, in addition, the "Oración Cívica" anticipates the constructive phase of Mexican positivism during its heyday in the entering era of Reconstruction, inasmuch as it closes with the optimistic remark that all the elements of "social reconstruction" are so well assembled that the current "peace and order," if maintained for some time, would accomplish by themselves alone all that remains to be done.[21]

A closer examination of the "Civic Oration" will enable us to see concretely how Mexican positivism is a variation of European positivism adapted to specifically Mexican conditions, rather than just its "restatement." Whereas Comte looked upon French liberalism as a negative force leading to chaos, Barreda on the other hand views Mexican liberalism as a positive force making for order and progress. Consequently, to justify the reforms of the victorious liberals, whose political leader was "the immaculate Juárez," the "Civic Oration" conveniently replaces Comte's social trinity of "*Love,* Order and Progress" with "*Liberty,* Order and Progress" (italics added). However, the latter is Barreda's motto on September 16, 1867, but it is not what he believes a year later in his official report against the adoption of a certain Liberal volume on morals (by Nicolás Pizarro) for use as a textbook at preparatory school. The later Barreda changes his tune and returns to the unsympathetic attitude of his French master towards the individualistic conception of freedom. As soon as that change occurred, his Liberal bedfellows became his Jacobin bedfoes, with the result that the "great Liberal Party" got split into two factions: radical and moderate. With this split—the radicals adhering to their old revolutionary principles and the moderates going the new way of positivism—there emerged the old problem of how to reconcile concord and liberty. But this is getting ahead of the story.

Very soon after his "Oración Cívica" and probably on the strength of it, the Mexican government under President Benito Juárez invited Barreda to form part of a commission to reorganize the entire system of Mexican education from top to bottom. Barreda was the brains of the commission and its recommendations were immediately embodied in the Education Law of December 2, 1867. The following year he founded and directed the Escuela Nacional Preparatoria, the educational headquarters of Mexican positivism during the last third of the past century. In fact, we are not exaggerating when we say that positivism in some form or other became, from that day to 1910 or so, the official philosophy of Mexico. Comte's dream had come true at long last in Mexico, if not in the United States; but, like so many philosophic dreams, it turned out to be a nightmare which would have been difficult for its French maker to have recognized as his own.

In order to understand how positivism as a philosophy acquired its official stamp in Mexico, we must take a look at her peculiar social situation around 1867. Mexican Independence was followed by several decades of intermittent war, civil and foreign (remember, for instance, the Texas fiasco in 1847). Though Benito Juárez, the candidate of the Liberal Party, was elected to the presidency of the Republic the year after the Constitution of 1857 was approved, the opposition party contested the election and civil war resulted. Next came the French invasion in 1861 leading to the proclamation of an empire under the Catholic Maximilian of Austria. (The United States was too busy at the time with its own Civil War to apply the Monroe Doctrine.) Near the middle of 1867, after the French troops were evacuated and Maximilian was executed, Juárez returned to power. But the Juárez who came back to the presidency in 1867 was not the Juárez of 1857. The interim of ten years had taught him, above all, the horrors of chaos and the dangers of extreme liberalism. Hence the slogan of his new presidential policy: *Peace* and *Order.* In short, given the chaotic circumstances of Mexico in 1867, it is not surprising that a moderate liberal government like Juárez's should have entrusted Barreda with the task of restoring social order through education.

The end of 1867, Zea points out, marks the transition from the "combative phase" of positivism to its "constructive phase." This transition is intelligible in terms of the political appeal to *Peace* and *Order,* the goal of which was to provide a stable economy to foster industrial development. The era of Reconstruction was on its way in Mexico and positivism was imported as its explicit *Apologia.* Without its official function as the ideological instrument of the up-and-coming middle class, positivism would have remained a purely academic affair in Mexico or a borrowed system of philosophy in Barreda's head.

As the prophet and theorist of "social reconstruction," Barreda saw that Mexico had to reconcile the conflicting interests of her social classes in order to attain national growth. He was practical enough to realize that in a country like Mexico political liberalism had to be controlled for economic purposes. As a Comtist, he argued that the romantic principles of the extreme liberals belonged to "ontological politics," which was a subtle way of telling them that their individualistic conception of liberty was incompatible with their economic goal, that is, self-defeating, inasmuch as it would ultimately lead to disorder. True liberty does not consist in doing what one pleases, but, to take his analogy from classical physics, just as a freely falling body is governed by the law of gravitation, so a freely acting person is governed by the laws of social order. In fine, though Barreda was a relativist concerning individual rights, he was an absolutist concerning social duties. Individual freedom, therefore, had to be made compatible with social security. Finally, he must have also realized that the lack of social unity in Mexico would make it easier for foreign interests, especially "the Colossus of the North," to capitalize on her internal struggles and make merry and money at her expense.

Like his French master, Barreda looked at philosophy in general as the instrument of social salvation and saw in positivism the specific instrument to reach that end. The Mexican disciple, however, was clever enough, being a lawyer-physician (he had been trained in both professions), to know that the Comtian medicine had to be prescribed so as to fit the particular conditions of the patient in question, his own sick country. The Positivist Catechism, in other words, had to be translated into Mexican terms to be intelligible and workable. Mexico, after all, was not France! Hence it was indispensable to take into account the Catholic roots of Mexican folkways. There was to be no Religion of Humanity *à la* Comte. This was too much for Mexico. The Church was to be permitted to conduct its spiritual business without interference, so long as it did not encroach upon the material affairs of the State. As to the State, its function for Barreda was to be simply "guardian" of public order. Therefore, he was against Comte's idea of state intervention or control of wealth. This compromising attitude of Mexican positivism explains why, in contrast to Brazilian positivism, it never opened a Church in Mexico and, even though Augustín Aragón, its surviving representative, has been nicknamed the "Positive Pope," Aragón is a Pope without a Church in Mexico.

The fundamental aim of Barreda's positivist program was to "destroy anarchy" in all its forms. Ironically enough, there was anarchy in his own backyard to contend with. That is to say, his old friends in the Liberal Party were undermining his educational policy with their "negative" spirit of individualism. Although he was willing to concede that they had done well with the job of defeating the clerical and the military, nevertheless he felt it was high time to get down to "positive" business and plan for the future, not just rest on the laurels of the past. To reconstruct Mexican society it was necessary to select leaders from the new middle class for training as philosopher-kings, or to be more exact, as scientist-kings. Barreda had a tremendous faith in a scientific education because he saw in its intellectual order the very "key" to the social and moral order which Mexico needed so badly. Using an economic metaphor typical of the nineteenth century, he argued that science with its reliable method of acquiring knowledge would issue in "a common fund of truths," which would guarantee a community of interests to offset the class conflicts within Mexican society. Away with Metaphysics! The Gospel of Science, not Jesus, will save Mexico!

So far so good, at least, on paper. But—there seems to be always a "but" in the story of mankind—what in fact happened was that all the talk about Science (with a capital S), which was proclaimed by the Mexican Comtists as the firm foundation for the reconstruction of a country in chaos, turned out to be mostly propaganda, since the only scientific discipline taken seriously into consideration was mathematics. As a matter of fact, the Comtian tradition in Mexico outdid Comte himself in that it made mathematics not only the foundation of all knowledge but also its *Summa.* Why so? Was Barreda so optimistic over its pre-established harmonies as to try to outdo Spinoza by urging the planning of Mexican society according to a geometric pattern? After all, Barreda was quite aware that the geometry of a good society requires more empirical stuffing than could ever be supplied by the beauty of Euclid alone. As a physician, he must have heard of Claude Bernard, his French contemporary who was revolutionizing medicine through the application of the experimental method. And lest it be thought that Bernard was not known in Mexico City then, we know from a reliable source[22] that the

(Mexican physiologist Ignacio Alvarado introduced Bernard into Mexico during the time that Barreda was directing the Escuela Nacional Preparatoria. Yet, knowing all this and probably more, why did he stress mathematics as *the* science of sciences?

The reason is more practical than theoretical. Barreda's political experience had taught him that only a neutral type of social reconstruction could bring peace and order to Mexico, and he knew as a positivist that a *neutral* science alone could provide the foundation for such a goal. Given a neutral end-in-view, a neutral means necessarily follows, he must have argued implicitly, if not explicitly. Who could accuse the mathematical kind of intellectual order, upon which was to rest the social and moral order, of being politically suspect? No, mathematics could never be attacked for being partisan! Barreda and his disciples, who organized themselves into a society called *Asociación Metodófila* and eventually published the *Revista Positiva,* must have known that only mathematics could legitimately fit in with their system of "uniform education," in spite of the fact that they talked so much about the application of the "positive method" to all fields of inquiry, from mathematics to sociology. Down deep in their hearts, if not in their heads, these scientific *methodists* must have realized that their quest for certainty could find no genuine satisfaction outside of the mathematical realm. How could they really believe their empirical method, however dependable, would lead to "sure" conclusions in the social field, as Porfirio Parra, Barreda's successor, claimed? And how could they prove from sheer observation that the rich are "superior" to the poor, let alone convince the latter that theirs was a neutral ideology set up for the social reconstruction of a country in chaos? In short, the very logic of the situation forced the Mexican Comtists to fall back willy-nilly on the neutral but irrelevant ground of mathematics.

The fundamental argument of Barreda's Mexico Compromise,

that positivism had to launch a neutral program in order to destroy anarchy in all its forms, was clever indeed but totally unconvincing to its opponents. For it did not take the opposition long to realize that its Neutrality Policy was not really neutral at all. Both the Catholics and the old liberals soon came to the realization that positivism, despite its loud claims of being a "neutral" doctrine, presumably of benefit to the nation as a whole, was actually a "sectarian" doctrine working only for the interests of a special class in Mexican society. That class, Zea keeps repeating, was to call itself "the Mexican bourgeoisie."

Viewed historically, Mexican positivism started as Comtian and ended as Spencerian. As Zea explains the change from one form of positivistic ideology to the other:[23]

> The generation of men educated by Gabino Barreda, those men who were to guide the nation along the road of progress, felt restrained in the ambit of Comtian positivism. Try as Barreda might, positive philosophy did not justify the freedom that most interested the middle classes: the freedom of getting rich without other limitations than a man's own capability. In Comte's philosophy individuals were subordinate to society in all material respects. This was the meaning of his *sociocracy* and his Religion of Humanity. Comte's politics and religion were not accepted by Mexican positivists, in contrast to those in Brazil and a group in Chile, because his political and religious doctrines were contrary to the end for which that philosophy in general had been adopted. That end, as pointed out before, was the formation of a middle class similar to that in England and in the United States.
>
> The theorists of the Mexican bourgeoisie were not long in discovering a doctrine fit to guide and to justify their actions; it was provided by the English positivists John Stuart Mill and Herbert Spencer (particularly the latter), and by the theory of evolution of Charles Darwin. The theories of those men appeared to mark the safest way and, at the same time, to coincide to a considerable degree with the ideas set forth by the first of the Mexican middle-class theorists, José María Luis Mora.

The period from 1880 to 1910 in Mexican history is usually named, after General Porfirio Díaz, Porfirism. The ideological counterpart of the Porfirist régime was a Mexican variety (or distortion, if you like) of Spencerian positivism. The political organ of the Mexican Spencerians was the newspaper *La Libertad* (1878-84) and their party went under the name of Unión Liberal. Its members looked at themselves as "new conservatives," *i.e.,* conservative liberals as against the radical liberals (the Jacobins) and the moderate liberals (the Juaristas). In 1892 the Liberal Party issued a manifesto supporting a fourth re-election of Porfirio Díaz and defending his régime on "scientific" grounds. (As a result, by the way, the opposition dubbed it the Partido de los Científicos.) What actually were these "scientific" grounds?

Two major arguments were presented by the Porfirists, one historical and the other theoretical. As to the first, according to Justo Sierra, the leader of the Mexican Spencerians and editor-in-chief of *La Libertad,* the fundamental moral to be drawn from the anarchic character of Mexican history was simply this: economic evolution is the indispensable condition of political evolution. Applying Spencer's interpretation of human history to Mexico, he tries to show in his popular book, *Evolución política del pueblo mexicano* (1902-03), that the decisive step in the political development of his country was taken when the *bourgeoisie* replaced the *caudillo* as the governing class of the Mexican people. The author submits that the passage from the military to the industrial stage of Mexican society came in the Era of Porfirism. With respect to the second or theoretical argument, the Mexican disciples of Spencer, who conceived liberty as something belonging to a *future* stage of social evolution, contended that the goal of political freedom could not be reached without its necessary prerequisite, public order. It should be noted that their idea of liberty was different from that of the Mexican Comtists, who put political freedom in the "metaphysical" or *past* stage of the human mind. This difference in the two groups of Mexican positivists came out sharply in their reaction against the Jacobin Constitution of 1857. For whereas the Barreda group attacked it as outmoded, the Sierra group criticized it on the opposite but more tactful ground of being untimely. Consequently, the latter argued that freedom from want is more important for an industrially underdeveloped country like Mexico than freedom of speech. In other words, if Mexico was to get on her feet as a nation and if she was to achieve Progress as well as Order—the two famous catchwords of that day—then economic freedom must be given priority over political freedom, the right to wealth over the right to vote. First things first!

As for the Jacobin appeal to the sacred Rights of the People, another contributor to *La Libertad* debunked them thus:[24]

> People are fed up with them; what they want is bread. To constitutions teeming with sublime ideas which no one has ever seen functioning in practice . . . they prefer an opportunity to work in peace, security in their personal pursuits, and the assurance that the authorities, instead of launching forth on wild goose chases after ideals, will hang the cheats, the thieves, and the revolutionaries . . . . Fewer rights and fewer liberties in exchange for more order and more peace . . . . Enough of utopias. . . . I want order and peace, albeit for the price of all the rights which have cost me so dear . . . . I daresay the day is at hand when the nation will declare: We want order and peace even at the cost of our Independence.

To have that "order and peace" at any cost in Mexico (the diabolical wish, unfortunately, came true) Francisco G. Cósmes recommended as an emergency measure the doctrine of an "honest tyranny." Here follows his apologetic for a dictatorship of the bourgeoisie: "Since we have gone on granting rights over rights which have produced nothing but misery and malaise, we will now try a little *honest tyranny;* let us see what that can accomplish." [25]

The *tiranía honrada,* as is well known, lasted not a little while in Mexico and each time that Dictator Díaz got himself re-elected (there were seven or eight), the so-called Party of the Scientists hailed him as the "honest tyrant." The Científicos, from Justo Sierra to Francisco Bulnes, managed to accomplish quite a deal, of course, but all for the vested interests of the ruling class, the Mexican bourgeoisie. They exploited Darwinian arguments to justify the ways of Porfirism to Mexican men. They had the audacity to affirm that the very survival of the powers that be signified that they were the fittest to govern the country. Along with the doctrine of "honest tyranny" for home consumption, they urged the "Sàxonization" of the Latin soul to compete with "the giant nation" growing by leaps and bounds across the border. Yes, the *Paz Porfiriana* had fully arrived in Mexico, but like its venerable ancestor the *Pax Romana,* it came with all kinds of strings attached. The Mexicans, like all other oppressed peoples in the world, had to pay the usual price for the Thirty Years' Peace guaranteed by force.

To recapitulate, the Mexican bourgeoisie during the larger part of the Reconstruction period had at the service of their ideals —political order and economic progress—a beautiful working team: positivism as intellectual tool and Porfirio Díaz as political "stooge."

So far, the ideological sides of all the major social classes in Mexico save one, the army, have been accounted for. As everybody knows, the history of Mexico is filled with famous and infamous episodes of the militaristic variety. And what is still better known is that generals when they are abroad in the land (in Mexico they seem to crop up overnight), do not go to philosophy as a handmaid, but rather resort to the hand grenade. So much for the obvious.

V. THE ANTI-POSITIVISTIC STAGE

Twentieth-century philosophy in Mexico began with a large-scale revolt against positivism. In the remainder of the chapter attention will be focused on the combative side of the story, the discussion of its constructive side being reserved for subsequent chapters. Before proceeding, however, I should explain why I have been obliged to have recourse to a negative label, "anti-positivistic," for an over-all description of the contemporary stage of the Mexican mind. The reason should be quite obvious: twentieth-century Mexican thinkers are in agreement with respect to what they are *against*—traditional positivism—but not with respect to what they are *for*. As it is too early to tell whether all of them hold some positive ground in common, establishing the nomenclature must be left to a future historian of Mexican ideas.

The Mexican revolt against the official philosophy of the Por-first government took shape as an organized movement during the first decade of the present century, that is, almost at the out-break of the Revolution of 1910. It would be an historical error, however, to suppose that positivism in Mexico had no critics be-fore the twentieth century. As a matter of fact, throughout its hegemony in Mexican education and politics, the positivists had to contend with the severe opposition of both the romantic liberals and the Catholic thinkers. Two examples from the first group are the Mexican Jacobins, José María Vigil and Hilario Gabilondo.[26] The first attacked positivism, ironically enough, on the ground of its being a doctrine of "anarchism," using the argu-ment that the heads of that school—Comte, Mill, Spencer—had not been able to come to terms with each other. Vigil, of course, goes to their polemical writings to prove his case. As to the second gentleman, Gabilondo was a disciple of the German philosopher Karl Krause, whose theistic system of metaphysics ("panenthe-ism") gained a popularity in late nineteenth-century Spain quite comparable to that of positivism in Mexico. In 1880 Gabilondo fought the positivists in the Liberal newspaper *La República* over the question as to which logic text was to be used in the National Preparatory School, their stronghold. The positivists suffered a temporary setback that year when the Mexican government issued a decree prohibiting the use of Alexander Bain's *Lógica* as official text, replacing it with the logic text written by G. Tiberghien, a Belgian disciple of Krause. Moreover, in itself evidence of opposition is the fact that Barreda's original Comtian program for the National Preparatory School, which he had meticulously planned, with presumably good intentions, for the unification of the Mexican mind on a scientific basis, was watered down to an eclectic orientation soon after he resigned from the directorship of the School in 1878. Nevertheless, in spite of all the criticisms which positivism received from the left and from the right during its heyday in Mexico, these never reached the momentum of the anti-positivistic campaign launched in the first decade of the present century.

The most significant feature of the Mexican revolt against traditional positivism lies in the unorthodox conception of philosophy which was implicit therein from the very beginning and which, as the last chapter will attempt to elaborate, was made explicit later by those ideologists who came to articulate the philosophical import of the Revolution of 1910. At the risk of repetition, two brief comments will serve here. First, regardless of the specific differences among the dominant schools in the previous stages of Mexican thought, all of them share the traditional view that philosophy is by nature a theoretical discipline whose object is to obtain eternal truths about the world and man. Secondly, more far-reaching in the long run than the immediate reaction against positivism on the part of contemporary Mexican thinkers is the final reaction of their most representative group against the traditional conception of philosophy itself. The notion they have come to accept may be denominated, after the Spanish philosopher José Ortega y Gasset, the "perspectivist" conception of philosophy.[27] It means essentially this: philosophy is not the quest for certainty, but rather the search for a *point of view* on human life. And as every point of view reflects a determinate climate of culture, philosophy is necessarily a contextual affair. In short, there is no philosophy in general for perspectivism; there is only philosophy in particular, *e.g.,* Mexican, etc. The obvious moral of the perspectivist conception of philosophy is that henceforth Mexicans should look at the world from a *Mexican* point of view and thus put into practice on a national scale the Socratic dictum: Know Thyself. With this anti-positivistic stage, philosophy has at last come of age in Mexico.

Since history requires dates, the year 1910 may be selected to mark the beginning of the contemporary period of Mexican thought. In that year a new society of young intellectuals called the Ateneo de la Juventud organized a series of lectures on the personality and work of Spanish-American thinkers and men-of-letters. Note the accent on *Spanish-American* culture, a reflection of the interest of the group in expressing themselves and not merely imitating European patterns. Six public lectures were delivered by its charter members at the National School of Law in Mexico City during August and September of 1910.

Of the six lectures sponsored by the Athenaeum of Youth, the last one given by José Vasconcelos, "Don Gabino Barreda and Contemporary Ideas," is the most pertinent to the present story. Vasconcelos starts off by giving Barreda credit for having established a better system of education in Mexico than Scholasticism, and admits that scientific fanaticism is more progressive and more in keeping with the times than religious fanaticism. But he quickly adds that positivism failed to realize that "the poetic sense" is not just a primitive stage of the human mind which the natural sciences have outgrown. Furthermore, Barreda was mistaken even on his own hallowed ground of Science, inasmuch as his dogmatic attitude towards it prevented him from seeing what the best authorities in the field knew, namely, that scientific principles are "mere hypotheses." Vasconcelos appeals to Poincaré, Carnot, Clausius, Lord Kelvin, and Bergson in his case against scientism. He closes with these telling words: "The positivism of Comte and Spencer could never satisfy our aspirations." [28] This lecture expresses so well the spirit and program of the Ateneo and the new intellectual generation of 1910 that it can be said to constitute the Mexican Declaration of Philosophical Independence.

The Ateneo de la Juventud was founded in Mexico City on October 28, 1909. Its first president was Antonio Caso. The membership came to fifty or so, a few of whom lived in the provinces, like Diego Rivera, the famous mural painter. The members came from all walks of life and the majority of them were lawyers by profession, including José Vasconcelos and Antonio Caso, the young philosophers of the group. Though the group was heterogeneous in composition, the members all had a common goal: to contribute to the spiritualization of a demoralized country. Their plan of action was to concentrate on those fields which had been sorely neglected during the reign of Positivism. The Ateneístas started among themselves an extensive reading campaign to prepare themselves for the task of cultural renascence. The reading program was carried out in two directions, one in literature and the other in philosophy. As to the first, they abandoned French nineteenth-century literature and plunged into the Greek classics, Dante, Shakespeare, Goethe, the Golden Age of Spanish letters and the modern trends of English literature. In philosophy their first attacks on Comte and Spencer were made with the anti-intellectualistic weapons of Schopenhauer and Nietzsche. All these readings helped them replace the Reform "spirit of 1830" and the Reconstruction "spirit of 1867" with other ideals.[29]

The Big Four of the Ateneo, its co-founders, were the late Pedro Henríquez Ureña, Alfonso Reyes, Antonio Caso and José Vasconcelos. The first was a native of Santo Domingo and the remaining three, Mexicans. The Mexican trio looked upon their Dominican friend as a sort of Socrates working behind the scenes. The four of them met at first in an architect's studio to plan the ways and means of spreading the "new humanism" throughout Mexico. As was psychologically natural, these young men of the Mexican *Sturm-und-Drang* started off by attacking positivism, each in his own manner. To quote Henríquez Ureña:[30]

> We felt the intellectual oppression together with the political and economic oppression which a large part of the country was aware of already. We saw that the official philosophy was too systematic, too definitive not to be mistaken. Then we embarked on reading all the philosophers whom positivism used to condemn as useless, from Plato, who was our greatest teacher, down to Kant and Schopenhauer. We even took Nietzsche seriously (imagine that!). We discovered Bergson, Boutroux, James and Croce.

Henríquez Ureña omits here what Vasconcelos had close to his heart, namely, Hindu philosophy and Oriental mysticism, an influence alien to the rest. Antonio Caso in his version of the same story reports that it was Kant's *Critique of Pure Reason* which helped them detect the epistemological error underlying all empiricism.[31] Nevertheless, of all the sources of inspiration behind the Mexican revolt against positivism, the subsequent evidence shows that Bergson was, on the whole, the most influential.

The series of public lectures under the auspices of the Ateneo in 1910 was not an isolated event in Mexico; it was rather the culmination of a number of intellectual episodes prior to it. This story would be incomplete without a word or two about its immediate antecedents.

The first public reaction of the Centennial generation against positivism was expressed in a student journal called *Savia Moderna,* which made its appearance in 1906. Alfonso Reyes gives Ricardo Gómez Robelo credit for initiating the attack. Gómez Robelo and the founders of *Savia Moderna,* Alfonso Cravioto and Luis Castillo Ledón, later joined the Ateneo. In the following year the Sociedad de Conferencias, the predecessor of the Ateneo, was formed by a select group of young rebels. Henríquez Ureña, on looking back, considers the year 1907 decisive in that practically all remnants of the positivistic way of thinking disappeared from the leaders of the campaign. But, even though the revolt was touched off by a small number of dissatisfied young men, it is fair to add that a man of sixty turned about-face philosophically and gave them an official pat on the back. That sexagenarian was none other than the Spencerian historian and educator Justo Sierra, who was at the time Porfirio Díaz's Secretary of Public Instruction.

On the night of March 22, 1908, Sierra delivered a memorable address at the Arbeu Theatre in Mexico City in honor of the chief propagandist of positivism in Mexico. But, as it turned out, the distinguished speaker gave Barreda no more than a left-handed compliment. For, surprisingly enough, he questioned the latter's conception of science as the "unquestionable" area of experience, with the result that from that moment on the official philosophy of Mexico was literally in crisis. With Sierra's agnostic temper as a Spencerian coming to the fore in his "Dudemos" address,[32] the very foundations of the positivistic school in Mexico were shaken by its own doubting Thomas. The schism between Spencer and Comte created by the Chief of Staff within the ranks was naturally exploited by the brewing opposition outside. So much so that it did not take long for the anti-positivistic forces to capitalize on the old military principle of *divide et impera*. Given this public disavowal on Sierra's part, it is no surprise that two and a half years later he patronized the Ateneo's series of lectures.

At this juncture it is pertinent to ask a question which recalls a general problem raised at the opening of the chapter. What is the relation between the Ateneo and the Mexican Revolution of 1910? To answer it adequately, one would have to solve the highly debatable issue as to what that Revolution is all about.

The Mexican Revolution, of course, has meant different things to different people and even to the same people at different times. To complicate matters, it is fairly well known that the Revolution began around 1910 as a political uprising to depose Dictator Díaz, but later developed in the hands of the Zapatistas, whose battlecry was "Land and Liberty," into an agrarian movement to get rid of private property. (Incidentally, Emiliano Zapata's movement was, to borrow Frank Tannenbaum's distinction, "communal" in nature, not "communistic"). Some are of the opinion that the Revolution was over long ago, while others insist that it has not really got into full swing as yet. One point is reasonably sure: the Revolution not only has meant different things to Masons and Marxists, to Catholics and Capitalists, but it has not even meant the same thing to its own políticos, from Madero to Cárdenas. Sceptics would be tempted to infer from all this that there is no use talking about the Mexican Revolution because one cannot discuss its facts without injecting his own point of view, but if one were to accept the sceptical position, a particular point of view in itself, he could not discuss any facts at all and the story would have to end abruptly.

Since the story must go on, come what may, the original question, in all its complexity, must be grappled with. To begin with the first of the two extremes in social theory, cultural parallelists would argue that there is no causal connection between intellectual and social events, and hence none between the anti-positivistic campaign of the Ateneo and the Revolution. Cultural interventionists, on the other hand, would argue that intellectual forces are, or at least can be, the direct agents of social changes, and hence the Ateneo was responsible for the Revolution. However, the truth of the matter, to recall what Russell rightly maintains, lies somewhere between these two extremes of the argument. Pedro Henríquez Ureña evaluated the Mexican situation well when he soberly remarked in 1927: "The Ateneo lived amidst battles and was, on the intellectual plane, the prelude to the gigantic transformation which was beginning in Mexico." [33]

To understand how the anti-positivistic wave of ideas sweeping the country in 1910 could be the prelude to the revolutionary movement in the making, one must bear in mind that positivism in Mexico was not just an academic affair involving professors alone, but the official philosophy of the Porfirist government. Henríquez Ureña and others of the Ateneo knew then from direct experience that positivism was, in the words of the Dominican humanist, "the ideological basis of the political tendencies in power." [34] Given the general feeling of unrest over the long dictatorship of Porfirio Díaz, the anti-positivistic campaign of the Ateneo was bound to affect eventually the very foundations of his régime. For in criticizing positivism directly the young rebels were indirectly attacking Porfirism. And once the theoretical foundations of the Porfirist system of politics were shaken by men of ideas, all that remained to be done, of course, was for men of action to finish the job. The men of action appeared in Mexico soon enough and have been in action and reaction ever since. Positivism and Porfirism were like Siamese twins, and the fate of the one followed as the night the day that of the other. Thus ended the ignoble experiment of Porfirism in Mexico.

From the foregoing it would be safe, in my opinion, to infer that the cultural leaders of the Ateneo were the intellectual fore-runners of the Mexican Revolution. They were not, however, its political directors. Their work led in part to the Revolution, but they did not lead it. Vasconcelos, in an autobiographical mood, has bluntly stated that there was "no atmosphere" [35] at the time for an intellectual flowering which might have given the Ateneo a rôle in public life. In fact, a significant difference be-tween the Mexican Revolution of 1910 and the Russian Revolution of 1917 is that intellectuals did not participate in the former as they did in the latter, unless we are to stretch the Mexican Revolu-tion beyond its military manifestation. By that token, of course, there is no fixing of dates. Madero, in any case, was no Lenin with a blueprint for revolution. All it seems he wanted for Mexico was a decent and workable government, and that is very difficult to plan anywhere, no matter how many years one has to do it in. His murderers gave him less than two years, which is too short a time to judge his success or failure as president. We can indeed speculate about what he might have done had he lived, but history is not usually patient with such speculative dreams. The leaders of the Revolution after Madero were far from belonging to the so-called "intelligentsia." Most of them were fairly ignorant and all of them were men of action who relegated men of ideas to secondary posts.

If the question is raised as to where the intellectuals of Mexico were in 1910, the answer is that the great majority of them, the old-timers, were Porfiristas and hence against the Revolution. As for the new ones of the Ateneo and their generation, they could have easily been dismissed by the men of action on the ground that they were too young to make any impression in public ad-ministration, but not on the ground that as intellectuals they would have refused to do their part in the national crisis. No, the Ateneístas, on the whole, would not have sympathized with that kind of "intellectual" who withdraws under the pressure of difficulties. Vasconcelos in *Ulises Criollo*,[36] the first of his autobiographical volumes, reports that during the Madero régime the Ateneo

> . . . was no longer the cenacle of lovers of culture, but the circle of friends with their eyes on political action. Antonio Caso was perhaps the only one who did not wish to get mixed up in the new situation. He proclaimed himself, more than ever, a Porfirist. Nevertheless, he collaborated in everything which signified cultural activity.

Caso, of course, changed his mind after the premeditated assassination of President Madero in 1913. Moreover, the Ateneo was not an organization of intellectual snobs who believed in restricting the treasures of culture to their small clique. In order to extend the radius of their program aimed at improving Mexican society as a whole, they founded, on December 13, 1912, the first Universidad Popular in Mexico, whose work in free adult education lasted ten years. The motto of the school came from the pen of Justo Sierra— "Science protects our Country"—which, naturally, they did not interpret in the traditional positivist fashion. After Madero's murder, unfortunately, the members of the Ateneo were dispersed by the ensuing fireworks and the meetings of this vitalizing institution came to a sad end.

At this point the connection between the Ateneo and the Revolution of 1910 becomes clear. Since the Ateneo's campaign against positivism "initiated the rehabilitation of the thought of the race," [37] as Vasconcelos put it, it follows that such cultural rehabilitation, which stems from that very campaign, is the ideological expression of the Mexican Revolution, insofar as we take that Revolution to signify a *discovery* of Mexico *by* Mexicans as well as a *recovery* of Mexico *for* Mexicans.

Now that the mediate and the immediate antecedents of the Ateneo, together with its Mexican Declaration of Philosophical Independence in 1910, have been sketched, it is fitting to take a brief look at the general effects of that call to intellectual freedom and spiritual autonomy on the educational life of contemporary Mexico.

On September 18, 1910, a week after the last lecture in the Ateneo series, the Díaz government at the request of Secretary Justo Sierra, the Spencerian who had already disavowed his positivist faith in 1908, reopened the doors of the University of Mexico. This act, in all probability a mere tactic on Díaz's part, turned out to be the best piece of administration ever sanctioned by the "honest tyrant" for the cultural life of his country during his Thirty-Year Iron Rule. What it amounted to in fact was the establishment of a new institution, *i.e.,* a *secular* university for the nation. It must be remembered in this connection that the predecessor of the National University, the Royal and Pontifical University of Mexico, had been closed since the stormy days of the anti-clerical Reform period. And when one considers that the original University, which had been patterned after that of Salamanca, held the signal honor of being the first institution of higher learning in the New World (antedating Harvard, to be exact, by eighty-five years), it should be no surprise to hear that the progressive elements in Mexican society welcomed Sierra's educational step with a touch of national pride and great expectation.

The reopening of the University on a secular basis was not mere sequence but consequence, so to speak, of the new *Geist* of the times rising phoenix-like from its positivistic ashes. With it, as an integral part, there was created the Escuela Nacional de Altos Estudios, which later became the existing Faculty of Philosophy and Letters. Philosophy was thereby reinstated in the university curriculum after having been in abeyance for more than seventy-five years in the state schools. (The private schools were the only places where speculative philosophy was being taught in Mexico during that period.) Lest this sound too surprising, it should be borne in mind that Barreda's National Preparatory School taught logic and morals but not philosophy proper, because the Comtian scheme relegated the latter to the so-called "metaphysical" stage of knowledge, thus leaving no room for it in the "positive" stage. Philosophy in the era of Porfirist Reconstruction had been restricted to bookish formulas of supposedly scientific sociology; and, as the converted Sierra metaphorically expressed it in the inaugural address he delivered at the opening ceremonies of the new University, the poor thing had been roving around academic halls pleading to be heard. The voice of metaphysics finally won its academic right to be heard once more at the University in 1910, and the next year that rejuvenated institution listened to Antonio Caso speak with all his personal eloquence in her behalf. Ever since then, philosophy's voice has become louder and louder in Mexico. It now looks as if she will no longer have to go pleading in that country, even though she has had to face opposition here and there in the interim, particularly from the Marxist group, in connection with Article Three of the 1917 Constitution, which prescribed a "socialist" system of education.

Finally, respects should be paid to the late Ezequiel A. Chávez, the grand-old-man of contemporary Mexican thought. Chávez, one of Mexico's most conscientious educators, used Spencer and Titchener to fill the gap left by Comte's omission of psychology as an autonomous science. He began his career in philosophy as a Spencerian evolutionist. Later on, coming under the influence of the anti-positivistic campaign in Mexico, he pitted Spencer against Spencer and to escape agnosticism, he read Bergson, Husserl, Descartes, Felix Ravaisson and a host of other philosophers. In 1935 his first philosophy book, *Dios, el universo y la libertad,* was published in Barcelona. This small volume revives Ravaisson's "spiritualistic positivism." [38]

According to Chávez, the right kind of positivism must be integral and take into account *all* the facts, psychical as well as physical. Traditional positivism is really *negativism* in that it denies some of the facts. The soul is as much a fact as the body and we know of its existence through intuition and love. That, in brief, was the way Chávez talked fifteen years ago. However, when the present writer had the pleasure of interviewing him a few months before his death in 1946, he defended orthodox Roman Catholicism. In the beginning Chávez called it Evolution, but in the end he called it God. His Catholic faith emerges unmistakably in his posthumous book, *De dónde venimos y a dónde vamos?* (1946), which is an *apologia pro vita sua.* One may, if he wish, wonder whence Chávez came and whither he has gone, but one thing at least remains clear, namely, that in his last testament he managed to find his way back to the fold and vision of the world which characterized Mexico's colonial times. Hence the course of his long life (he died at almost eighty), intellectually considered, is that of Mexico writ backwards.

3

The Christian Dualism
of Antonio Caso

I. BIOGRAPHICAL NOTE

Antonio Caso y Andrade was born in Mexico City on December 19, 1883. He received all his formal education in the schools of that city, attending the Escuela Nacional Preparatoria, where he studied psychology under Ezequiel A. Chávez and history under Justo Sierra. After being indoctrinated into orthodox positivism at the National Preparatory School, he went to the Escuela de Jurisprudencia for his training in law and was graduated with the traditional degree of *licenciado*.

In the preceding chapter mention was made of Caso's rôle as one of the Big Four in the anti-positivistic movement of the Ateneo de la Juventud. On the reopening of Mexico's University as a national institution in 1910, he was appointed its first professor of philosophy, a position which he held, along with teaching sociology in the Law School, practically until his death. Though his academic life was interrupted at various intervals by the shifting winds of politics, his long years of devoted service to teaching earned for him the title of *el Maestro* of contemporary Mexican thought. So much so that one of his compatriots aptly described his work in the teaching profession as an "apostleship." In his last position he was engaged as lecturer at the Colegio Nacional, the highest institution of learning in Mexico, established by presidential decree in 1943 and patterned after the Collège de France.

Maestro Caso was essentially an orator-philosopher in and out of class, giving eloquent flesh to the idea that the history of philosophy is the deepest drama of life. Like Bergson, his master-philosopher, he held his large circle of listeners, including the ladies, spellbound with his exuberance and wit. If any reader is still looking for an excuse to learn Spanish, here are two prize examples of Caso's play on the *m*'s:

No me gustan las masas ni las misas: prefiero las mozas y las musas.

La 'm' es letra peligrosa porque es la inicial de la mujer, la música y la metafísica—mis tres vicios.

Antonio Caso was the recipient of many national and international honors. The degree of *doctor honoris causa* was conferred upon him by his own alma mater, the University of Rio de Janeiro, San Marcos and Guatemala. He lectured at the Universities of San Marcos, La Plata, Buenos Aires, Chile, Rio de Janeiro and Havana. He won decorations for distinguished service from various countries, among which were France, Chile and Peru. He was not only a great teacher inside and outside of Mexico, but served his country as ambassador to Peru, Chile, Argentina, Uruguay and Brazil.

As educational administrator, Caso held the following posts in Mexico: Head of the National Preparatory School, Secretary and later Rector of the National University, Director and finally Honorary Director of the University's Faculty of Philosophy and Letters. He was founder and president of the Centro de Estudios Filosóficos, the Mexican counterpart of the American Philosophical Association. He was associated with the following learned societies: the Academia Española de la Lengua, the French Academy, the International Institute of Sociology, the Academia de la Historia of Colombia, and the Academia Nacional de la Historia of Buenos Aires.

Antonio Caso died suddenly from a heart attack on the night of March 6, 1946, one day before he was scheduled to begin his series of lectures on "The Problem of the Philosophy of History" at the Colegio Nacional. The Mexican Socrates passed away quietly and Mexico wept.

II. EARLY STAGE OF CASO'S THOUGHT

Three stages may be discerned in the development of Caso's philosophy, which he was fond of describing as "a Christian vision of the world." [1] These stages are as follows: (1) the anti-intellectualist, (2) the pragmatist, (3) the dualist.

Caso's first book, an introductory text entitled *Problemas filosóficos,* was published in 1915. This work shows more than anything else the tremendous influence of the Bergsonian conception of intuition on his intellectual formation. Notwithstanding his appeal to intuition, his methodological position at the time is ostensibly eclectic. "To arrive at metaphysical truth," he states, "it is necessary to combine the methods and results of science with the truths of intuition." [2] Yet, though he pays lip-service to the function of reason as a useful tool for survival, his heart is really set on intuition as *the* way to metaphysical knowledge. And after paying his respects to Schopenhauer's metaphysics based on experience, he champions Bergson's *Creative Evolution* and its speculative vitalism.

Following his French master, the early Caso was a double anti-intellectualist in the sense that he was an intuitionist in metaphysics and a pragmatist in science. There are seeds of the pragmatic conception of science in the *Philosophical Problems* of 1915, but they do not sprout till four years later when he published his main work, *La existencia como economía, como desinterés y como caridad* (title hereafter abbreviated). Not that Caso in 1919 loved Bergson less in metaphysics, but he loved James more in science. (The two loves naturally go together for any double anti-rationalist.) So much so that the Mexican author emphasized their common distrust of reason, rather than their positive differences in methodology. "The anti-intellectualism of the present day believes," he said with approval, "that man is neither a simple contemplator of aesthetic forms, nor a singer of the harmonies of the creation, nor an *epiphenomenon* of the world, but an actor, an inventor, a creator." [3] In short, his ideal of man is the Bergsonian-Jamesian *homo faber,* not the Spinozistic *homo cogitans.*

III. CASO AS PRAGMATIST

The early Caso, as we have just brought out, was a half-pragmatist in methodology, *i.e.,* a pragmatist only with respect to *scientific* truth, but the middle-aged Caso was a complete pragmatist in that he applied the test of utility to *all* truth. In order to make intelligible his defense of the pragmatic theory of knowledge, one must look at the middle period of his life. The dedicatory page of his monograph, *El concepto de la historia universal* (1923), laconically refers to that time as one of trying days for all. What he is driving at in all probability is the chaotic aftermath of the Mexican Revolution of 1910, not to mention the general disillusionment arising out of the failure of the Wilsonian dream to make the world safe for democracy. We know from other sources that José Vasconcelos was at the time Minister of Public Education under the Obregón régime. As Vasconcelos went up in national esteem, it seems that Caso went down. This is one of the perplexing stories of the contemporary Mexican scene. In any case, whatever the social and personal circumstances may have been, the middle period of Caso's thought definitely expresses, to borrow a phrase from Gilbert Murray, "a failure of nerve." What are the specific manifestations of his strange interlude as a Christian pragmatist?

In the 1919 edition of his essay on *Existence,* Caso is a pragmatist only as far as science is concerned. On the other hand, *The Concept of Universal History* of 1923, which outlines various philosophies of culture, preaches complete pragmatism in theory of values, making truth a value subject to the same criterion as the useful, the good and the beautiful. Admitting that his axiology gets its inspiration from the French sociological school of Durkheim, he calls his view "social objectivism." [4] According to this view, the objectivity of value is determined by society. The essence of value is whatever satisfies or tends to satisfy a collective desire. No society, no value. Thus utility is whatever is *socially* useful. And by extension, truth is whatever is *socially* true; goodness, whatever is *socially* good; beauty, whatever is *socially* beautiful. The author considers *el objetivismo social* the true compromise between the ontologist thesis, which holds that values are independent of the valuer, and the subjectivist antithesis, which argues that values depend completely on the individual.

The pragmatic bent of Caso's mind in the middle period of his life gets neatly epitomized in a nine-point intellectual autobiography published in a collection of essays in 1922, *Ensayos críticos y polémicos.* The *Confessio Fidei* is called *Mi convicción filosófica.* Its agnostic variety of Christian pragmatism speaks so well for itself that I shall translate the whole of it. If one should be surprised at the sudden resurrection of Herbert Spencer in what follows, Caso would remind him, as he reminded one of his outspoken critics as late as 1927, that positivism "continues to influence my philosophic conviction down to the present." [5]

MY PHILOSOPHIC CONVICTION [6]

by ANTONIO CASO

1. We are in the world *to work*. We do not know the nature of our action and probably shall never know it; yet the meaning of our efforts is intelligible.

2. The positive sciences and history are perfectible disciplines, which with each advancement will make more intelligible our efforts to control the world and ourselves.

3. In contrast, there is almost no metaphysical progress. Not one of the great cosmological theories of the pre-Socratics has been surpassed or excluded, for that matter, from the group of contemporary metaphysical ideas. Hylozoism is still a way of conceiving the ultimate nature of reality. For it is through this naïve assimilation of spirit and matter that the philosophical thought of Greece began.

4. Logic, ethics and æsthetics, in other words, practical philosophy (*canon*, as the Stoics used to say, the rule of human life, the *philosophy* of value, as we moderns say) has entered fully into an era of definite progress. Logic is essentially an *economic*, biological, utilitarian affair. It is the learned and parsimonious form of egoism. Mach, W. James, Bergson, Poincaré, etc., are the epistemologists who have solved the problem of reason as far as reason *can;* that is, they have solved the problem of the law of rational *behavior*, whose *forms* were permanently established by the Greeks, especially by that eternal prince of true thinkers, as Comte calls Aristotle of Stagira. For the *nature* of thought will always be an enigma to thought itself, as Höffding wisely and eloquently teaches at the end of his Compendium on Psychology. In short, we know *how* reason functions and *why* it does so, but we shall never know *what* it is. *Docta ignorantia.*

5. Kant, the greatest philosopher after Aristotle, was the founder of æsthetics. To him we owe these impeccable definitions: "the beautiful is disinterested pleasure" and "purposiveness without purpose." Schopenhauer and Bergson perfected the theory by *deintellectualizing*

it, so to speak; they got rid of its Platonic element. Plato was the best philosopher of the poets and the greatest poet of the philosophers.

6. Our Lord Jesus Christ founded ethics. As long as there was nobody to sacrifice himself for the ideal of sacrifice, ethics remained simply a matter of *theory,* that is, metaphysical talk as ingenious and profound as you wish, but still theoretical, dialectical and unreal. Socrates died not to be inconsistent with himself; Jesus died through spontaneous inspiration. He did not think, like the Greek, in syllogisms. He lived. Christian morality is living, not hypothesis; action, not law; conduct, not imperative. I should have liked it had Jesus never existed or, if so, had he not sacrificed himself; or had he manifested himself in his century as an angel, a spirit, or a supernatural phenomenon. But he was a *man* and therefore, since we are men, it is necessary to be like him. There is no way out. In dying on the Cross, he made us all accountable. If we don't sacrifice ourselves, we don't save ourselves. This is the truth.

Buddha the inspired, the other great religious founder besides Socrates and Jesus, died from indigestion caused by truffles. If the moral world is will, the falsest of moral hypotheses is the negation of the will to live.

7. Through education we bring about the realization of the whole man. This means that we are an ideal entity which has not reached complete maturity in History. To imitate Christ (not in the way of that famous medieval book where the contempt of the world is taught), but as St. Francis of Assisi imitated him—this is human destiny. To create men who are good and shining spirits, dynamic centers capable of artistic disinterestedness and moral abnegation (Charity)—this is the Law and the Prophets summed up in the love of one's neighbor as oneself.

The rest, cosmology and ontology, are shams of human reason, which does not exist for understanding the essence or substance of anything, but for the sake of action. Reason serves action through: (1) Scientific knowledge, building up Industry, which is always progressive, as against Metaphysics, which is always unprogressive; (2) Ethical knowledge, developing Man as the only attainable purpose of the world and history; (3) Aesthetic knowledge, relieving us of the pain of living with the pleasure of seeing and hearing for their own sweet sake.

8. At the bottom of all things there is something, I know not whether Omnipotent, but certainly noble, loyal and humane, which makes possible the heroism and sacrifice required for achieving a goal; and perhaps I can only have a glimmer of it on the condition that I humble myself before that Being and realize that I cannot understand it.

9. Our Father which art in heaven, hallowed be Thy name, Thy will be done on earth, as it is in heaven. Give us this day our daily bread. Forgive us our debts, as we forgive our debtors. Lead us not into temptation, but deliver us from evil. Amen.

IV. CASO'S CHRISTIAN DUALISM

From the confessions of a Christian pragmatist in twentieth-century Mexico, attention falls next upon Caso's final position in philosophy. In order to determine the nature of that position it is important to consider it in relation to his master, Henri Bergson. But before Caso can be connected with Bergson, Bergson must first be related with himself.

The late philosopher from Paris reported in his last major work entitled *Les deux sources de la morale et de la religion* (1932; English trans., 1935) that its mystical conclusions "complete naturally, though not necessarily, those of our former work,"[7] *L'Evolution créatrice* (1907; English trans., 1911). This distinction between a natural and a necessary completion which Bergson makes with respect to the development of his philosophic position, however vague in the context of *The Two Sources of Morality and Religion,* is significant for the purposes of indicating Caso's possible originality in philosophy. A close study of *Creative Evolution* and *The Two Sources of Morality and Religion* would show that "the impetus of love" stressed in the latter does not necessarily follow from the general doctrine of the *élan vital* emphasized in the former. Perhaps the best test case of their difference in tone is Bergson's rather subtle shift in his idea of God.

In *Creative Evolution,* God is defined as "unceasing life." But in *The Two Sources of Morality and Religion,* God is defined mystically as "love." The author, of course, tries ingeniously to develop the second notion out of the first. Nevertheless the two propositions—"God is life" and "God is love"—are a projection, in his case at least, of opposite attitudes towards life. The first reflects an attitude of ultimate *attachment* to life; the second, in contrast, one of ultimate *detachment.* The first is entertained by a man who has illusions about life; the second, by a disillusioned soul. Evolutionists, *e.g.,* the early Bergson of *Creative Evolution,* hug life so much they call it God; mystics, *e.g.,* the later Bergson of *The Two Sources of Morality and Religion,* shrug their shoulders at life and appeal to something superior, to wit, spiritual love. (Psychologically speaking, of course, the attitude of detachment usually comes after that of attachment simply because the process of disillusionment a man undergoes presupposes the possession of prior illusions.) In short, Bergson the mystic is not really consistent with Bergson the evolutionist. In other words, the doctrines of "creative evolution" and "complete mysticism" are not ultimately congruous in temper. For biological and religious romance do not mix very well.

Be that as it may, one thing is clear from *The Two Sources of Morality and Religion,* namely, that its author is applying the methodological principles of *An Introduction to Metaphysics* (1903; English trans., 1912) and *Creative Evolution* to the field of morals, politics and religion. The outcome of Bergson's intuitionism is what he calls "complete mysticism," his final position in philosophy. And this is where Antonio Caso comes into the picture. A comparative study of the 1919 edition of his essay on *Existence* with *The Two Sources of Morality and Religion* would disclose that its "Christian vision of the world" is more consistent with religious mysticism than Bergson's metaphysical biologism, where "all morality, be it pressure or aspiration, is in essence biological." For the central idea of Caso's thought is that Christian *caritas* is the "mystical victory"[8] over life in the biological sense. Accordingly, all genuine morality is in essence *anti-biological,* inasmuch as the kind arising out of social pressure is not morality at all for Caso but simply economy. Before developing his thesis, one must try to trace it back to its origin.

The germ that was to mature in Caso's mind goes back to at least the year 1915, when he was in his early thirties. That year proved to be very crucial for the young Mexican, because it was then that he gave a series of lectures on the "great Christians" at the Ateneo's Universidad Popular Mexicana, out of which the first draft of his Christian vision of the world was born. The original manuscript was published the next year (1916) in pamphlet form (41 pages) under the title *La existencia como economía y como caridad,* with the subtitle *Ensayo sobre la esencia del cristianismo.* The essay was expanded to 153 pages in 1919 and its title was changed to the one we have already mentioned, *viz., La existencia como economía, como desinterés y como caridad,* the subtitle being removed. But this is not all there is to the story of his essay on *Existence.* A new edition, of 199 pages, appeared in 1943 under the same title as that of 1919. A careful comparison of the two editions reveals no substantial change in philosophical attitude. Besides a revised preface and a new preliminary section called *Sub Specie,* the last edition differs from the previous one in only one important technical respect: it subtracts James, adds Husserl and reinforces Bergson with Driesch. In other words, the sympathy for pragmatism drops out considerably and intuitionism returns in full force, with the Husserlian intuition of essences supplementing the Bergsonian intuition of existences. In short, Caso ends as a *double* intuitionist in methodology.

In *Sub Specie,* the new two-page foreword to the 1943 edition of the essay on *Existence,* Caso presents in a neat fashion his idea regarding the nature of philosophy. Philosophy is defined as the attempt at a "synthesis"[9] of the different points of view from which existence can be considered. These points of view are as follows:

(1) *Sub specie aeternitatis*—the metaphysical point of view.
(2) *Sub specie durationis*—the historical point of view.
(3) *Sub specie utilitatis*—the economic point of view.
(4) *Sub specie charitatis*—the moral point of view.
(5) *Sub specie relationis*—the logical point of view.
(6) *Sub specie pulchritudinis*—the aesthetic point of view.

The six aspects of reality, the last four of which are a faint echo of Croce's famous "four moments of the spirit," according to Caso, contain on analysis three major antinomies: (1) the metaphysical versus the historical; (2) the economic versus the moral; (3) the logical versus the aesthetic. Consequently, the task of philosophy, as he sees it, is to find the synthesis that will solve the above antinomies.

Before an examination of Caso's particular synthesis in his essay on *Existence,* note should be taken of his shift in position with respect to the nature of philosophy. In those trying days of *Mi convicción filosófica,* metaphysics was supposed to be all "humbug." This agnostic conception of philosophy, however, finally gives way to the traditional view that philosophy is the attempt to give an explanation of reality. All is not vanity any longer in cosmology and ontology, except the vanity of any dialectic which fails to see that existence is more complex than any theory with unilateral formulas dreams of. To be sure, absolute knowledge still remains an ephemeral illusion, but the world is intelligible just the same. Philosophy is no longer the handmaiden of action; she is now the humble servant of truth. Thus our author in the end returns to the ancient tradition of *philosophia perennis* and regains his original faith in philosophy as the synthesis of knowledge. His agnostic bark had been greater than his bite.

If one grants with the mature Caso that philosophy is the synthesis of the six aspects of things, the aim of which is to resolve their conflicting claims, what is its necessary condition? "The philosophy of our time," it is insisted, "must be founded on experience; it must, however, be founded on *all* experience, that of the laboratory and that of the oratory." [10] In a word, the required synthesis must start with experience *as a whole*.

The Mexican author, to repeat, calls his own synthesis "a Christian vision of the world," but an examination of the content of the essay on *Existence* shows that the proposed *Cosmovisión cristiana* is an unfinished synthesis. Only three out of the six aspects—the economic, the aesthetic and the moral—are discussed in any detail. Of the three antinomies that philosophy is asked to reconcile, one alone receives serious attention, the economico-moral. Reference to the other three aspects and to the other two antinomies can be culled here and there in the book, but they are nowhere developed. Nor is his monograph on *The Concept of Universal History,* whose thesis is derived from Croce, any help in the solution of the historico-metaphysical antinomy. Yet, even though Caso's unfinished synthesis is not at all analogous to Schubert's *Unfinished Symphony,* it may be said in his favor that half a synthesis is better than none.

Why does Caso concentrate on the great antinomy of Life versus Charity? And why does he write against life in the biological sense? The reason is obvious enough. Like so many of us, Caso has lived through two World Wars and the editions of his principal book register his reaction against what he calls "the philosophy of imperialism," which puts animal life above law, greed and power above justice and love, the self-centered individual above the respect for human personality. That reaction is unmistakably recorded in the two companion volumes appearing during World War II, *La persona humana y el Estado totalitario* (1941) and *El peligro del hombre* (1942), both of which attack individualism and communism as rival "forms of egoism" and defend the Christian conception of politics.[11] Is it any wonder, then, that Caso devoted most of his intellectual energy to writing an apologetic for Charity in an age when the creed of biological exaltation and the cult of violence were on the rampage? Any decent man would want to do that very thing in a world filled with inhumanity, even at the expense of repeating the wisdom of the age and the sages.

The Christian view of man is given its metaphysical setting in the essay on *Existence*. The aim of the essay is to justify anew the ways of God to contemporary man. Caso, however, is neither a St. Augustine nor a John Milton. Yet he is fully aware that, in a period when the Nietzschean-inspired cult of Life for Power's Sake has been so popular, it would be quite useless to write a Christian *Apologia* unless there were good philosophical reasons in its favor. The faith of our fathers will not do. It is philosophy that must come to the rescue and meet the devotees of animal life on their own ground. A metaphysics based on experience must, of course, respect all the conclusions of biology, but such acceptance does not commit it necessarily to a mechanistic interpretation of *all* life. In short, biology, yes; biologism, no!

What are, according to Caso, the philosophical reasons in support of the Christian view of the world? They are the well-known arguments of *neovitalismo* found for the most part in the works of Henri Bergson and Hans Driesch. A consistent vitalism, one based on all experience, in contrast to the materialistic or naturalistic view of the world (materialism and naturalism are both reductionist for Caso), affirms not only the irreducibility of life to matter, but also believes in the existence of another order of reality which is irreducible to the vital economy and thus distinguishes man from the beasts. The author adopts the contemporary type of metaphysical dualism on the authority of the neo-vitalists and sociologizes it thus: "Culture is opposed, logically, to Nature." [12] This Culture-versus-Nature duality clearly reflects the influence of sociology, rather than biology or psychology, on his philosophic formation. In a word, his specific brand of existential dualism is Nature and Culture, not Nature and Life, nor Nature and Mind.

The essay on *Existence* is divided into three parts, dealing with the world as life, as art, and as morality.

According to Caso, the essence of life in general (meaning life on the biological plane) is economic or utilitarian in character. The idea comes from Arthur Schopenhauer, the terminology from Ernst Mach. Wherever there is life, there is economy: the vital = the economic. To explain the nature of the vital economy pervading the organic world, Caso proposes the following hypothesis: "*vital energy,* that original irreducible reality which Driesch treats of, *is conscious or unconscious egoism.*" [13] It is unconscious in the beast, conscious in man. Caso's hypothesis of "the egoist entelechy" is obviously no more than an Aristotelian name for the Darwinian struggle for existence interpreted in neo-vitalist terms. What is egoism? The egocentric predicament is not simply an ethical or epistemological problem in the human world, but a "non-spatial metaphysical principle" operating throughout the whole area of life and determining its evolution. This principle is supposed to be self-evident to intuition, that is to say, "not born within experience," [14] a conclusion which is incompatible with the general empirical appeal proclaimed in the Preface. In any case, the full equation of pure life *ut sic* is: the vital = the economic = the egoistic. Appropriating Bergson's statement in *Creative Evolution* that each member of the species aims "only at its own convenience" and "goes for that which demands the least labor," [15] Caso formulates the fundamental equation of the universe *sub specie utilitatis* as follows: life = the greatest profit for the least effort. [16]

The counterpart of the economic conception of life is the economic theory of knowledge. The last two editions of the essay on *Existence* accept the first view, but both reject the second ("epistemological utilitarianism") in its extreme form, that is, when the pragmatic test is applied to *all* truth. It is at this point in the 1943 edition that the author gives up the agnostic pragmatism of his confessional days around the early 'twenties. No counter-confessions appear, however, nor is the personal change of heart reported. Nevertheless, it is clear that the 1943 edition is completely sympathetic to the "rectification" of the agnostic point of view. One has only to compare the 1919 edition with that of 1943 to get the rather subtle shift of attitude with respect to pragmatism in general. [17]

Edmund Husserl is the new philosopher whom Caso appeals to in the last edition to refute those who reduce all knowledge to utility. Yet, despite the fact that he praises the phenomenological movement for its "revindication" [18] of the rôle of intuition in the apprehension of essences and values, it is really Bergson whom he understands, not Husserl. Probably his weakest book is *La filosofía de Husserl* (1934). He cannot "see" Husserl as well as Bergson, nothwithstanding all the lip-service to the "ideational act" in his companion volume with that title, *El acto ideatorio* (1934). And strange as it may sound to a strict Husserlian, Caso's reading of the literature on the subject of phenomenology leads him to the dubious conclusion that there are four "irreducible forms" of reality: bodies and minds, essences and values.[19]

In order to make the bridge from Nature to Culture, the essay on *Existence* exploits the Bergsonian notion of "a surplus of energy"[20] in the world of living things. Caso holds that the origin of science, art, morality and religion goes back to this surplus energy available in human conduct. Not that these forms of human culture are reducible to purely vital force. Even though the higher animals are likewise supplied with an excess of energy, they have no culture. For they use up all their energy for practical purposes and thus remain brutes. Brutes are always pragmatists, but men can sometimes be saints. Hence surplus energy is the necessary condition of culture, but not its sufficient condition. In view of the duality of origin, a new anti-economic principle is needed to explain the arrival of man as against his survival. That metaphysical principle, which is neither deducible from the organic world nor reducible to it, is called "disinterestedness," a Kantian category in Schopenhauer and Bergson incorporated into Caso's synthesis. We are now in the universe of art.

The world *sub specie artis* is a world of *desinterés*. On the other hand, the world *sub specie vitae* is characterized by self-interest. Each member of the organic world is struggling to save its own skin with as little effort as possible. But the biological imperative of least effort cannot explain the "innate disinterestedness" of human life *qua* human. Although the laws of biology can doubtless explain many traits of existence, they cannot explain all of them, *e.g.,* the birth of art, inasmuch as the fine arts run counter to the economic or egoistic motive of life. Art is not even play, as Schiller and Spencer after him thought, because play is a definite part of the economy of life. Animals play in order to survive; men instead cultivate art for its own sweet sake. (Incidentally, Caso admits that play is the closest thing to art in the vital economy.) What is art, then? Art is, in Kantian terminology, "disinterested pleasure," or pure contemplation of the world, as Schopenhauer insisted. The most interesting feature of Caso's conception of art, in my opinion, is that through the emergence of art existence sheds its animal flesh and the human spirit is born. Art and man coexist. With the advent of art, this simian world acquires humanity itself.

After telling us what art is in the second part of the essay on *Existence*, Caso turns to the question of its method. Art is not accessible to pure reason. To reason is to relate terms. But whence the terms? The answer given is Bergsonian: the terms come from intuition. Through intuition contact is made with the concrete particulars of reality. The method of art, in a word, is intuition in the Bergsonian sense or "aesthetic intuition," [21] by which is meant the apprehension of individual terms. Whereas the scientist thinks abstractly, the artist intuits concretely. Artistic genius is, therefore, the ability to express the individuality of things, such as a Iago or a Mona Lisa. It is obvious that Caso would sympathize with all those who believe in the cognitive significance of art.

Caso tries to solve the antinomy between intuition and reason by considering the two sides of the conflict in method as complementary aspects of knowledge. "Reason and intuition complement each other." [22] Intuition is the first stage of inquiry, reason the second. Under logic, the rational or relational aspect of existence, is included material as well as formal science, both of which yield *universalia* in varying degrees of abstraction. For Caso, logic is truth and beauty is truth, but unlike Keats, we need to know *both*. Nevertheless, of the two kinds of knowledge, Caso really favors the intuitive. For he states: "Thinking is only tolerable when one can't see." [23] In other words, an Aristotle is only tolerable when one can't be a Dante. As to his general epistemology, Caso takes for granted the realistic doctrine that the objects known are independent of the knower. No critical discussion of the epistemological problem as such is to be found in any of his publications.

Just as the first form of existence, the realm of Nature, is subdivided into two autonomous orders—the physical and the biological—so its second form, the realm of Culture, is subdivided into two equally autonomous orders—the aesthetic and the moral. "There is not one order alone but *various orders*, involving their mutual contingency." [24] Each order is irreducible, governed as it is by its own laws. (This accent on the "contingency" of the laws of Nature and Culture derives from Bergson's immediate precursor, Emile Boutroux, to whom Caso dedicated his 1917 essay on "Contemporary French Philosophy.") Moreover, considered from the axiological point of view, the world is an ordered hierarchy of values, ranging from the physical to the moral. The physical order is beyond good and evil; the biological order is evil; the aesthetic order is neither good nor evil but neutral in value; the moral order is good. All of which leads to the conclusion that Caso's main interest in the nature of things is not to know them as such; it is rather to evaluate them from a humanist standpoint.

The essay on *Existence* assigns a metaphysical place to art in the normative scheme of things. That place lies "midway" [25] between the biological and moral orders of existence. Art, being disinterested in character, breaks the cosmic law of the selfish will to live and thus prepares the way for the flowering of moral will. Art as "inaction" is the intermediary through which man can pass from organic to spiritual action. Although disinterested contemplation is the forerunner of morality, a society of artists would be quite ineffective. For art is only the "will-less" order of things, thanks to Schopenhauer. Action at its best is altruistic action. With an act of sacrifice the moral world is born in all its splendor.

As one would expect, Caso's dualistic vision of the world reaches its culmination in the final part of the essay, which treats of *la existencia como caridad.* The author not only performs a transmutation of values opposite to Nietzsche, "the great German Sophist," but also a transmutation of categories akin to Jesus. Love is more than the fulfillment of the law; it is the fulfillment of existence itself. "The world as charity," the author keeps saying like a refrain, "is reality in its fullness." [26] Hence *The Moral Economy* by Ralph Barton Perry would be a contradiction in terms for Caso. He would argue that the proper title of the book should have been *The Vital Economy.* For the moral order is the anti-economic principle of existence *par excellence.* Morality is to be defined in ascetic terms, as sacrifice, not in utilitarian terms, as interest. The basic equation of the moral life is the antithesis of life on the organic level: sacrifice $=$ the greatest effort for the least profit. [27]

A morality based on interest, according to Caso, is egoistic or centripetal. It is morality only in name, but immorality in fact. The Mexican author does not concern himself at all with the old paradox of egoism versus altruism, or with the problem of the quality of interest involved. All self-interest for him is intrinsically evil. He believes, so to speak, that the egoistic motive makes the organic world go around at the expense of making the moral world go down. The history of man is like St. Augustine's *Tale of Two Cities,* one "based on egoism," the other "built on Charity." [28]

What is meant by love or *caritas?* At its best it is more than the Golden Rule preached by moralists; it is the way of life of any person, like Jesus, who sacrifices himself out of love for mankind. One could call it the Diamond Rule: do *more* unto others than you would have them do unto you. Is it fact or fiction? "Charity, like struggle, is a fact." [29] It is not something to be proved; it is something to be practised. It is precisely what all moral heroes do. Charity *is* as charity *does*. "Just as there is no seeing for the blind and no hearing for the deaf, so there is no morality and no religion for egoists." [30] He who does not experience sacrifice cannot understand the world as a whole. For just as we need the postulate of the uniformity of nature to explain physical phenomena, so we need the postulate of "the uniformity of charity" [31] to make spiritual phenomena intelligible. In fine, the altruist is not only a better man than the egoist; he is a wiser man as well.

Caso's moral outlook represents a positive type of absolute asceticism whose symbol is the Cross of Jesus. It does not, however, subscribe to Kant's jural type of ethics. The good is not a categorical imperative for the Mexican author. We should not be moral out of respect for rational law or out of a sense of duty, but out of enthusiasm. From this it is obvious also that the moral standard is no longer the "social objectivism" of the middle period of his thought. Goodness is determined by one's inner conscience, not by outer society. Virtue is the work of a "new instinct" deanimalized. As *der Wille zur Macht* (Nietzsche) is pure life, so *der Wille zum Guten* (Alfred Weber) is pure love. In other words, since Caso identifies Schopenhauer's intuition of life with Nietzsche's "impetus of power," the self-centered "will to live" defines, on the one hand, the biological order of existence and the self-less "will to love" [32] characterizes its moral order on the other.

Is there a distinct idea of religion in Caso's attempt at a synthesis of Christianity? Actually, most of the time he does not distinguish between morality and religion. So much so that he flatly declares: "The essence of Christianity is charity" and, more emphatically, "There is no God without good works." [33] His attitude toward religion is essentially that of a liberal mind. Caso, one must remember, was not an orthodox Catholic; he belonged among the heterodox. His patron saint came from Assisi, not from Aquino. Whenever he does distinguish religion from morality, it is defined in mystical language as a supernatural order characterized by the beatific life and everlasting peace. The religious order of existence, however, is not considered a fact, but a possibility beyond this world. It is admittedly an article of faith, not a tenet of philosophy.

The essay on *Existence* closes with a few comments on the Kantian theme of God, Freedom and Immortality.[34] The prospect for human immortality lies in the possibility that since the good man can survive in space, he may be able to survive in time. Two types of life—the biological and the moral—coexist in man, but their coexistence does not imply that the first is the sufficient condition for the emergence of the second. The biological order, to be sure, is indispensable as the cosmic support of moral life, but life as such does not constitute the good life. The death of animal life does not mean necessarily the death of moral life. The chances of our surviving death, however, ultimately depend on the existence of a supernatural order, inasmuch as even the moral order itself shall perish eventually along with the other three orders—the physical, the biological, the aesthetic—coexisting at present. The end of the world is inferred from the physical law of entropy. Nothing but pure spirit can ever expect to overcome the perishable nature of things. In any event, immortality is only a prospect for those who deserve it, that is, for those who have been disinterested and charitable enough during their life on earth. All the rest are doomed to utter extinction.

As to freedom, its essence is self-determination. Drops of

water have "individuality," but only human beings are capable of "personality" (a distinction reminiscent of Miguel de Unamuno). Self-determination means self-denial for Caso. We are truly free only when we deny our individuality, which is another word for egoism. The real person is the man who goes out of his way for others and turns the other cheek if necessary. To paraphrase a verse from St. Matthew: "He that findeth his life shall lose it; and he that loseth his life for charity's sake shall find it." In short, not *veritas* but *caritas* shall make us free. All the philosophies in the world are worth nothing in comparison with the altruistic action of a man of good will.

The discussion of human personality leads the Mexican author to his idea of God. From the fact that some human persons are at least good some of the time, it is possible to conceive of a Divine Person who is good all of the time. That Person is God. Thus God could not possibly be a Supreme Genus, as the pantheists believe, because a logical abstraction is no less barren when it is applied to the Deity than when it is applied to Humanity. The *Deus* of a Spinoza could not die on the Cross; Caso's Supreme Person can. If one asks the latter, where is God? *In nobis,* of course. If we have charity, we have God. For, in accordance with the Gospel of St. John, God is Love. It is vain to look for the Supreme Being elsewhere. In other words, Caso's God is conceived in the image of the humanistic personalist, who makes the highest in human value coincide with the fullest in existence.

By way of summary, Caso's Christian dualism can be placed against the background of the contemporary scene. Antonio Caso was of great service to the Mexican mind both as a dramatizing expositor of Western thought in general and as a Christian interpreter of Bergson's philosophy in particular. Technically speaking, his metaphysics adds virtually nothing new to the old debate of vitalism versus mechanism, except the multiplication of unnecessary entities. For one thing, Caso was not a trained biologist and his scientific information was second-hand. Nevertheless, the most significant feature in his treatment of the *antinomia profunda* between life and love is to be found not in the fact that he was defending a Christian vision of the world, which after all is nothing new, but in the fact that he was attacking the devotees of Life (with a capital L) at a time when they were fashionable in theory and in action. That time is our immediate past, a period "red with tooth and claw."

It is instructive to note why Caso's Christian vision of the world is dualistic. Having reacted against the Darwinian-Spencerian conception of Nature and its political expression in Mexico (remember Dictator Díaz, the "honest tyrant"), two distinct ways were accessible to him. One was to reject the positivistic arguments of the "tough Darwinians" in the last century on the ground that they were based on one-sided premises concerning the process of evolution. (Incidentally, since leading biologists[35] nowadays stress the natural principle of cooperation more than the struggle for existence, we might refer to them as "soft Darwinians.") The second way was the alternative Caso happened to choose, *i.e.,* to accept the egoistic premises of traditional Darwinism as true in biology but false in ethics. Thus he was obliged to assume some extra-biological entities grouped under the term Culture—*desinterés* and *caridad*—in order to compensate for the havoc wrought by the operation of the "egoist entelechy," the extra-physical postulate he concocted for organic nature by joining together Darwin's "struggle for life" and Driesch's "entelechy." Hence his *double* dualism in metaphysics: (1) between inorganic and organic nature on the one hand and (2) between Nature and Culture on the other. Had the Mexican author been better acquainted with contemporary biological theory, he might have become a Christian monist, like Vasconcelos, instead of a Christian dualist.

At all events, whatever we may think about the validity of Caso's plea for Charity, we must at least admit there was a touch of pathos and heroism in his defiance of that Nietzschean-inspired "impetus of power" which prides itself in looking down on Christian morals as an apologetic for the weak.[36] Life as such to Caso is nothing to brag about. We should therefore not make a virtue out of biological necessity. In spite of his being an eloquent disciple of Bergson's, he deserves considerable credit for never eulogizing his master's *élan vital*. And in contrast to Nietzsche, the German yea-sayer to Life, the Mexican thinker is a nay-sayer. His message, in brief, is life for love's sake, not life for life's sake. Not pure life, but the *good* life: the *abundant* life of Jesus. We do not have to escape *from* reality to be saintly, as Schopenhauer believed; we may escape *into* reality. For to live charitably is to experience the plenitude of existence itself. Caso's message is indeed as simple as all that. In its simplicity lies its nobility; and, needless to say, everybody knows from Spinoza that all things noble are as difficult as they are rare. Finally, whether Caso's attempt at a "synthesis of Christianity" is really such or rather just an eclectic combination of the Christian point of view and contemporary vitalism, *that* remains an open question, of course.

4   The Aesthetic Monism
       of José Vasconcelos

I. BIOGRAPHICAL NOTE

A biographical sketch of Don José Vasconcelos is quite super-fluous in the light of the fact that he has packed the details of his odyssey into four thick volumes.[1] Unfortunately, however, the autobiography of this Mexican author, who personifies himself as the "Creole Ulysses," is not available as yet in English, but that very appellation, though derived from what is an epic in form, can serve as a vivid reminder of the tragic sense of life pervading the Latin-American soul. It can also be used for the purpose of bringing to our attention the fact that Vasconcelos is not the academic type of philosopher. He has wondered and wandered too much to be a fitting academician. He does not really belong in spirit to the genteel tradition of our professors of philosophy. Rather, he has looked back at himself as destined by God to be a philosopher in the Platonic sense. Not that he can be accused of rationalizing his situation because, as a matter of fact, he has been honored with several important academic posts, including Secretary of Public Education twice in Mexico, Rector of the National

University of Mexico, Visiting Professor at the University of Chicago and of La Plata, and Lecturer at Mexico's Colegio Nacional. One reason for his anti-academic attitude is that professional teaching bores him to death; he once confessed not being very good at it. In this respect he and Antonio Caso are poles apart. Nor does he take much stock in honorary degrees. When the present writer interviewed him in Mexico City in 1946, he mentioned casually that he had been the recipient of three or four doctorates from Latin-American universities, but he could not even remember their names. Fortunately, *Who's Who in Latin America* (ed. P. A. Martin) contains the information that he received the *doctor honoris causa* from the Universities of Chile, Puerto Rico, Salvador and Guatemala. Like the great majority of the intellectuals in Latin America, Vasconcelos finds it necessary to divide his energies in order to make ends meet. At the time of our interview, he was lecturing at the Colegio Nacional, writing for publishers, newspapers and magazines, heading a private preparatory school, and directing the National Library of Mexico. If anybody thinks Mexicans are lazy, let him just consider what Vasconcelos does for a living.

José Vasconcelos Calderón was born on February 27, 1882, in the city of Oaxaca, Mexico. Though the first volume of his autobiography goes under the title of *Ulises criollo*, he should have called it, to be more exact, *Ulises mestizo* on the ground that, according to his own confession, there runs a "small amount of indigenous blood" [2] in his veins. After completing elementary school in Oaxaca, he went to Mexico City and attended the Escuela Nacional Preparatoria. On finishing his studies at the National Preparatory School, he registered as a law student in the Escuela de Jurisprudencia, obtaining in 1905 the licentiate degree in law. His thesis, *Teoría dinámica del derecho,* was published two years later in the *Revista Positiva,* the moribund organ of the Mexican positivists on the verge of becoming a target of the Ateneo de la Juventud. The young Vasconcelos had no further academic training; virtually all the philosophy he knows was self-taught and, indeed, self-thought.

Vasconcelos practised law for a while after graduation and in 1908 joined Madero's political club, the purpose of which was to stop the re-election of the dictator from his native city, Porfirio Díaz. In this connection he edited the anti-Díaz newspaper *Antireeleccionista* and spent a year or so in Washington as a confidential agent for the Mexican Revolution in the offing. When Madero was elected president of Mexico in October of 1911, Vasconcelos declined a political post in order to protect the new experiment in Mexican democracy from the accusation of nepotism. He returned to the legal profession, but his political experience and his reading of Plato's *Republic* inspired him to extend the law beyond the courts of private justice to a just state for his country. He took philosophy so seriously and Plato so literally that he aspired to be philosopher-king of Mexico. Being a Christian socialist at the time, he agreed as a socialist with Karl Marx that the task of philosophy is to change the world, but as a Christian he disagreed with the latter's materialistic proposal for doing so.

Vasconcelos got his first real chance at changing not the world but Mexico in 1920, when President Obregón appointed him to the cabinet as Secretary of Public Education. The Secretary on Horseback, as he was nicknamed when he held the same post for a very short time in 1915 under President Eulalio Gutiérrez, reorganized the whole educational system of Mexico and tried like a missionary for four years to raise the level of the Mexican mind— so much so that he can legitimately be honored with the title of Father of Popular Education in Mexico.

It is, of course, true that many jokes have been told about his persistent efforts to improve the educational conditions of his country, such as the now proverbial one about the distribution of Spanish editions of the classics among illiterate Indians in the rural areas. But, even if we grant the quixotic character of some of his educational experiments, there is no doubt that Vasconcelos as a "traveling salesman of culture" was a true son of the Mexican Revolution in that he did something concrete to bring its slogan of "Mexico for the Mexicans" out of the arena of political words into the realm of cultural works. The most striking evidence of his contribution to Mexican culture is to be found in the mural movement to which he was midwife in the early 'Twenties. It must not be forgotten that, to whatever extent he has since disowned his own children, the modern art movement in Mexico did not get public support until after he became Secretary of Education in 1920. The philosophy behind that movement was that drawing, for example, is more important than the methods of teaching it.

The general basis of the Vasconcelian reform of education directs its main animus against Dewey's pragmatic theory of education. In *De Robinsón a Odiseo*[3] (1935), he raises the ever popular debate between vocational training, symbolized by Robinson Crusoe, and liberal education, the symbol of which is Odysseus. He contends that Dewey's accent on "all learning by doing" produces the Robinsonian type of man and that the so-called "new school" is only an application of Anglo-Saxon "Protestantism carried to pedagogy." Since Mexicans are culturally Latins, it is argued that they can not and should not be trained in accordance with the inductive methods of the Anglo-Saxon way of thinking. Hence the primary need of the Mexican school system is to form a "new Odysseus," a type of man who will not be trained in knowledge for power, but rather will learn to enjoy ideas for their own sweet sake.

Although this is not the place to elaborate upon the Mexican author's theory of "structural pedagogy," one can seriously question whether such a philosophy of education is consistent with his general philosophy of civilization, especially that part which draws attention to the engineering needs of Latin America. Vasconcelos knows only too well that Mexico and her neighbors have to learn "by doing," but he simply hates to admit it. To admit as much is as difficult as it is rare. So much for the educational point of view of the Mexican "Ulysses."

To go back to the brief story of his eventful life, Don José was not quite satisfied with being philosopher-secretary under a military ruler. He wanted naturally to be a philosopher-president in his own right. His second and last chance came in 1929, the year he defied the powers that be and ran on the "anti-reelectionist" ticket against the stooge of Boss Calles. Pascual Ortiz Rubio defeated the "guiding light for all Latin America" without meeting much opposition. The losing party contested the fairness of the election, but to no avail. The upshot of it all was that instead of moving into the presidential palace, Vasconcelos was forced to move out of the country, thus becoming Mexico's most dishonored and disillusioned exile. This was not, in fact, the first time he had gone into exile, but it was the last. The Mexican "Ulysses" dropped his ambitious mission to be philosopher-king and turned thenceforth to the less disconcerting mission of being simply philosopher. His refrain since then could be put in the famous words of Henry Clay a century ago: "Sir, I would rather be right than be President."

In retrospect, Don José feels it is quite a miracle that he is still alive, given all the infamous intrigues of Mexican politics. He must have undoubtedly had some rather narrow escapes, but the very fact of his survival indicates that he was not such a dreamer after all. He knew how to duck at least. Like Aristotle, who had remembered what Athens had done to Socrates, he always managed to leave Mexico City in time so as not to let her sin even once against philosophy. Furthermore, with all the alleged bitterness over his political failure that his critics have thrown up to him, there is definitely one thing about which he is not bitter. He does not complain about his four or five exiles because, for one thing, they gave him an opportunity to read and write philosophy that he never would have had in his own country. The roving philosopher still recalls with a touch of nostalgia the many stimulating hours he used to spend at the Library of Congress in Washington and at the Fifth Avenue Library in New York.

One may, if one likes, accuse Vasconcelos of rationalizing his political failure, but we cannot accuse him of going to intellectual seed on account of it. For what Vasconcelos lost in politics he more than made up for in philosophy. The year 1929 marks both the end of his political career and, as we shall see, the beginning of his philosophical system. To those cynics who are prone to laugh at the Mexican "Ulysses," let them remember that Plato's *Republic* is located, after all, "in the sky," which is a poetic way of stating that the perfect city cannot exist on earth. Sooner or later every philosopher discovers the inevitable gap between the actual and the ideal Syracuse.

II. VASCONCELOS COMPARED WITH CASO AND BERGSON

Although Antonio Caso and José Vasconcelos were the philosophical twins of the Ateneo who joined forces to bury a decadent positivism in Mexico shortly after the *fin de siècle,* from the very beginning of their spiritual formation it can be seen that they were not identical twins. For one thing, the two young men were temperamentally different. Caso was tender-minded, conservative and professorial in his demeanor; in contrast, Vasconcelos was tough-minded, radical and academically heterodox. The first was satisfied with fighting "the philosophy of imperialism"; the second attacked imperialism itself, especially in its "Yankee" form. Whereas Caso played safe as a theorist, the Mexican "Ulysses" was too much of a man of action to rest content with theory alone.

Both Caso and Vasconcelos began their intellectual careers as enthusiastic followers of contemporary French philosophy, especially that of Bergson. As the previous chapter showed, the first not only started as a Bergsonist, but finished that way. In fact, one can really call Caso the more consistent version of Bergson in Mexico in that his Christian vision of the world and, in particular, his dispraise of Life, are more compatible with the cherished goal of the Paris philosopher: "complete mysticism." But Caso was too much a dualist to feel at home with the mystic's One. On the other hand, Vasconcelos, the "first stage" of whose thought was, to quote from his memorial article on Bergson, "doubtless Bergsonist," [4] has gone further than his French master in that he is an unashamed mystic. After all, the famous author of *The Two Sources of Morality and Religion* makes his appeal to "mystical intuition" with some mental reservations about its reliability for yielding knowledge.

Before a specific consideration of how Vasconcelos has gone beyond Bergson, the general comparison of the two major contemporary philosophers of Mexico must be resumed. The very name of the Vasconcelian system, "aesthetic monism," should serve for the time being to differentiate its *monistic* character from the *dualistic* feature of Caso's Christian synthesis. Furthermore, though both thinkers defend a Christian view of the world, Caso interprets it in *ethico*-religious terms; Vasconcelos does it in *aesthetico*-religious terms. For the former, art is *twice* removed from ultimate reality; for the latter, it is hardly *once* removed. To be more exact, the Casist hierarchy subordinates art to morality; the Vasconcelian does it the other way around. In other words, these two Christian philosophies represent the differece between the generalized perspective of an appreciator of morals on the one hand and that of an appreciator of the fine arts on the other.

A critical comparison of Bergson with Vasconcelos necessitates raising the crucial question as to whether that French philosopher was a monist or a dualist in metaphysics. Vasconcelos definitely defends an "existential monism" and consequently his philosophy as a whole is directed against dualism, but there is some doubt as to where the philosopher from Paris stands on this issue. Many interpreters regard Bergson as a dualist; however, those who emphasize his vitalistic strain, in which even matter is derived from life, see him as a panvitalist and hence as a monist. If one traces this difference in interpretation back to the original sources, he will find that two distinct elements, the mystic and the scientific, are responsible for his being, respectively, a monist and a dualist at the same time. The best proof of the instability of the Bergsonian system may be found in its last testament, *The Two Sources of Morality and Religion*. There Bergson *almost* works out a thoroughgoing monism which he denominates "complete mysticism." I stress "almost" because he actually fails to reach his proposed goal, despite his claims to the contrary.

A comparison of two fundamental passages from the aforementioned text proves this point. Bergson argues on one page against the materialistic possibility of reducing life to physico-chemical terms and concludes thus: "If life cannot be resolved into physical and chemical facts, it operates in the manner of a special cause, added on to what we ordinarily call matter." Yet, later on, this obvious duality of origin of life and matter merges into a mystic unity of life, because "spirituality" and "materiality" may be said to be "complementary aspects of creation." [5] Note the unconscious shift from a substantival analysis of metaphysics in the first passage to its adjectival analysis in the second. When Bergson talks of life and matter, he speaks the language of dualism; on the other hand, when he talks of spirituality and materiality, his language becomes monistic. The trouble with him is not only that he does not sense the difference between these two ways of speaking, but that he does not see clearly enough that the second way *alone* is compatible with a "complete mysticism." The first way, postulating the twofold origin of life and matter, can only lead to a unity of creation by miracle or *ex machina*.

Part of Vasconcelos' originality with respect to Bergson resides in his having removed the dualistic residue from the latter's metaphysics by insisting on a "rigorous monism." In addition, he has deintellectualized the Bergsonian conception of intuition. According to Bergson, intuition is "intellectual sympathy"; for Vasconcelos, on the contrary, it is "super-intellectual" sympathy: *pathos* or *emoción*. Finally, the two men not only differ in metaphysics and methodology; they differ even more radically in practical philosophy. Unlike Bergson, Vasconcelos thinks with Schopenhauer that the goal of human conduct is "to transcend life," not "create" it.[6]

In this last respect Vasconcelos is like Caso, who looks down on life by conceiving it *sub specie utilitatis*. Yet, in spite of their common moral aversion towards life in the biological sense, there is no doubt that Vasconcelos, though often erratic, has a more creative mind than Caso, or, for that matter, than any other thinker in Latin America. There are, to be sure, more scholarly *pensadores* in Mexico and elsewhere, but scholarship is not identical with originality of thought. And whereas the historical significance of Caso's Christian vision of the world lies in having anticipated somewhat the mystical position of *The Two Sources of Morality and Religion,* the merit of Vasconcelos' "aesthetic monism" lies in having insinuated what their French master would and should have said there had he carried out the logic of his proposed "complete mysticism" to the very end.

To summarize the comparison of the three philosophers under consideration, one might say that while Antonio Caso was a Mexican Bergsonist, José Vasconcelos is a Mexican *neo*-Bergsonist. It is to be hoped that the prefix "neo" will serve as a tag to differentiate conveniently the two most outstanding thinkers in Mexico inspired by Bergson.

III. THE ANTECEDENTS OF THE VASCONCELIAN SYSTEM

There are three antecedents in Vasconcelos to his system of Aesthetic Monism. These are *Pitágoras* (1916), *Monismo estético* (1918), and *La revulsión de la energía* (1924). But his law thesis, *Teoría dinámica del derecho,* dated April 30, 1905, demands attention first.

The Dynamic Theory of the Law deals with the general nature of justice from a Spencerian standpoint. Having been bred on orthodox positivism, its author defends the view that legal rules are an application of the law of conservation of energy to social phenomena. Law in society exists in the state of "potential energy" and thus ready for use whenever the opportune moment arises. The dynamic equilibrium resulting from the enforcement of a legal system produces in the people living under it a sort of "mystical feeling."[7] The foregoing phrases (*energía potencial* and *sentimiento místico* in the original Spanish) acquire great metamorphosis in the subsequent thought of our author. His intellectual career starts with a dynamic theory of the law *à la* Spencer and ends with a dynamic theory of reality *à la* Bergson.

The initial germ of Aesthetic Monism is to be found in an essay entitled *Pitágoras,* originally published in the September and October 1916 numbers of *Cuba Contemporánea,* an Havana monthly, and printed there the same year in booklet form. Its second edition was enlarged and published five years later in

Mexico City. Note should be taken here of the most interesting coincidence in the bibliographical history of contemporary Mexican philosophy. Both Caso and Vasconcelos published the original draft of their thought during the year 1916. The essay on *Pythagoras* is to the Vasconcelian "system" what the essay on *Existence* is to the Casist "synthesis." The difference, however, is that the former work constitutes merely the seed of what was to develop later into a full-fledged system of philosophy, while the latter expresses practically all there is to the philosophy of its author. Caso may have had the advantage in the beginning of being a Minerva in philosophy, but he had the disadvantage of having to repeat himself in the end.

Vasconcelos' *Pythagoras* is a masterpiece of ingenuity. It makes a mountain of interpretation out of a mole hill of source materials. Everybody knows that the information we have of the Pythagorean tradition is fragmentary, not to say legendary, but this state of affairs does not at all deter the Mexican "Ulysses" from offering a rather novel and daring interpretation of its number theory, to wit, "the aesthetic interpretation."

What, in brief, is the aesthetic interpretation of Pythagoreanism? It holds that the so-called number theory is really " a theory of rhythm," not a theory of mathematics. Now rhythm means alternating as against uniform motion. The Pythagorean number symbolizes the rhythmic movement of things everywhere, within ourselves and out in the spheres. Rhythm, in a word, is "process"; Pythagoreanism is a process philosophy. Therefore, the Pythagorean doctrine, that reality is numerical in character, should not be taken literally, that is, mathematically, but figuratively, as the very music of the spheres.

Since the basic category of reality, according to Vasconcelos' view, is rhythm, he reaches the bold conclusion that Pythagoreanism is in essence an "aesthetic," not a "mathematic" as tradition holds, nor an "ethic" as Schleiermacher believed. In other words, Pythagoras was the son of Dionysus, not the son of Apollo. That he had illegitimate children in his immediate disciples, who, like Philolaus, got away from "Pythagorean aestheticism," is regretfully admitted. Perhaps even the master himself, he adds with chagrin, may have fallen for the mathematical line as the path of least resistance, thereby missing the great chance of working out an aesthetic conception of the universe.

Whether Vasconcelos has discovered the secret of Pythagoras or not, the important thing for the present purpose is that where his Pythagorean treasure lies, there lies his heart also. For his heart is at bottom mystic and the Pythagorean sense of rhythm is to him the point of departure of all philosophical mysticism. In fact, he falls so much in love with the aesthetic interpretation of his subject that he sees it where it is not. Modern science, he claims, has confirmed Pythagorean thought "to a certain extent," but he misses the whole point that what it has confirmed is precisely the mathematical import of that tradition. He has even tried recently to find support for his ingenious thesis in Whitehead, the explicit defender of "the Pythagorean tradition of Mathematics" in *Adventures of Ideas*. (Incidentally, he not only misunderstands Whitehead, but, unfortunately, misquotes him.[8])

The essay on *Pythagoras* is the first sign of the author's dynamic vision of the world baptized in aesthetic terms. Using Bergsonian tools, he contends that the traditional view of the number philosophy fails to understand the rhythmic relations of the Pythagorean system of numbers on account of its intellectualist approach to the subject. Whereas science via intellect provides us only with useful abstractions in discourse, art via intuition supplies us with significant concretions in experience. Intuitive knowledge is "the aesthetic perception of things." Since the philosopher is considered an artist on a grand scale, philosophic method has to be synthetical, not analytical. Here are the roots of the methodology of Aesthetic Monism, which is developed in the *Tratado de Metafísica* (1929) and receives completion in *Lógica orgánica* (1945). There is, however, an important difference between the original statement of the Vasconcelian method in the *Pitágoras* and its final form. The early work defines the aesthetic approach to the world in Schopenhauerian language (of Kantian origin): "disinterested contemplation." The quality of disinterestedness is removed with revenge in the later works, perhaps as a reaction to Caso's emphasis on that quality usually attributed to art.

A closer examination of the relation of Aesthetic Monism to the essay on *Pythagoras* would reveal that Vasconcelos extracts the *aesthetic* feature of his system from Pythagoras, but he gets the *monism* from Plotinus, the great mystic of Alexandria. Not that he is Pythagoras plus Plotinus or even the product of the two. Vasconcelos is Vasconcelos! What one looks for, of course, is the original source of inspiration in the making of his mind. Of these two influences, Plotinus is the more important. So much so that the watchword of the *Pythagoras* is: Back to Plotinus! This *retorno a Plotino* is really the master-key to the philosophy of Vasconcelos. On looking back, Vasconcelos has frequently said that his system is "derived from Neo-Platonism." In the last few years, however, his sympathies reveal a return to the Roman Catholic Church, the original faith of his childhood. And instead of Plotinus, the palm goes to the Christian neo-Platonists, Origen and Clement of Alexandria. But whether the names change from Plotinus to the latter, the spirit of his thought remains the same; the change of names is, we suspect, practical in import, not theoretical. At any rate, Vasconcelos is no more a Thomist at present than when he swore by Plotinus. As a matter of fact, the latest hero of the Mexican "Ulysses" is Empedocles, who is taken to be the first philosopher in Greece to advise us not "to reduce quality" to quantity.

After he had put away the childish things of his positivist days in that famous Ateneo Manifesto of 1910, the basic problem for Vasconcelos was to construct a monistic system of philosophy which would not have the shortcomings of the "materialistic monism" typical of the last half of the nineteenth century. Nevertheless, the Vasconcelian temper showed from the start more of a revolt against metaphysical dualism than against materialism for the obvious reason that the latter at least believed in *one* world.

According to the Mexican author, Pythagoras was monistic enough to envision the inner and the outer world as rhythm, but he did not see what Plotinus later came to teach us, namely, that the rhythm of the one is opposite in kind to that of the other. Not that these two kinds of rhythm belong metaphysically to "two separate orders," two mutually exclusive worlds. No, dualism is categorically declared "insoluble." For its doubling of things into matter and force, body and soul, etc., makes the *univ*erse unintelligible. Vasconcelos calls the spiritual type of rhythm "Pythagorean" and the material type, "Newtonian." To put this distinction in his own words:[9]

> ... Nature is governed in the phenomenal order by the law of causality, and in the spiritual order by the Pythagorean rhythm of the disinterested and the beautiful. The *Newtonian* and the *Pythagorean* are the two necessary poles of everything thinkable: the material order of necessity and the spiritual order of beauty.

Or in terms of his pet metaphor of the "spiral," the difference between the two kinds of processes is one between a "closed" and an "open" spiral. The former is circular, that is, symbolic of necessity. (Note that the Vasconcelian polarity between necessity and beauty is analogous to the Kantian one between necessity and freedom. Whereas Kant, however, limits science to make room primarily for morals, Vasconcelos does the same thing to make room for beauty.)

The Vasconcelian system of philosophy was publicly announced for the first time in a small volume of essays carrying the title of the name of the system, *El monismo estético* (1918), published two years after the appearance of the *Pitágoras*. These essays were preparatory to a system of "aesthetic Metaphysics" that actually matured eleven years later in the *Tratado de metafísica* (1929). The volume as a whole contains the nucleus of Aesthetic Monism and thus serves as a general introduction to it.

Vasconcelos introduces his position with the general remark that the time has come to construct philosophical systems on the basis of the "mystery" of aesthetic judgment, rather than by the traditional means of pure or practical reason. As to why he adopts the name of "aesthetic monism," his explanation is that the unifying principle of science, morality and art is to be found in Kant's special feeling of beauty. The first part of *The Critique of Judgment* therefore constitutes for Vasconcelos the real prolegomena to all future metaphysics. So much so that this Mexican "Ulysses" dreams of a treatise on *Fundamental Aesthetics* comparable to no less than Spinoza's *Ethics,* but more in keeping with the times. Incidentally, the treatise he envisages is to be written in the language of the ear, not of the eye. For the ear is not only the best of artists; it is also the best of philosophers. Hence the trouble with Plotinus is that he was an "eye" mystic. Exploiting Schopenhauer's theory of music, Vasconcelos as an "ear" mystic and analogist speaks eloquently, if not convincingly, in behalf of what he christens "Auditory Mysticism."

According to *Aesthetic Monism,* philosophy should adopt "the method of music," since music is *the* art that best expresses the "concrete universal" of which Hegel speaks. Conceptual logic is too abstract to seize the concretions of existence. The aesthetic method, not the scientific method, is the golden key to metaphysical knowledge. The aesthetic approach to things is defined as the "super-intellectual" manifestation of consciousness, not anything impulsive or "sub-intellectual." In other words, aesthetic judgment goes beyond pure and practical reason, but not against them. So much for the preliminary statement of the Vasconcelian way of knowing.

As to his metaphysical point of departure, the author turns Kant upside down and transforms his idealist principle of "supersensible unity" into the realist conception of "substance." From the latter category of ancient philosophy to that of "energy" in modern science is an easy step for Vasconcelos. Scientific experience leads to a dynamic monism, that is, to a monism of energy. Energy is the scientific analogue of rhythm. As the world exhibits two kinds of rhythm, physical and spiritual, so there are two forms of energy. (Later on, Vasconcelos becomes "trinitarian" about the forms of energy.) All matter is energy, but not all energy is material. Since the total disappearance of energy is impossible, given the first law of thermodynamics, we must therefor assume that this energy passes into a latent but real state which is identical with the invisible "energy of our souls." The sages of the *Upanishads* "foresaw" this energist hypothesis long before the advent of modern science. The reference just made to the great Hindu classic recalls the deep influence of Indian mysticism on the formation of Vasconcelos' mind. The effect of such an influence can be readily seen in the sympathetic survey of Hindu thought he published under the title *Estudios indostánicos* in 1920. In fact, it is no exaggeration to say that his system of philosophy is a sort of meeting of East and West writ small. (Interestingly enough, a decade before the publication of *El monismo estético,* William P. Montague of Columbia University presented a scientifically neater and better developed case for the same energist theory of mind in his William James paper, "Consciousness a Form of Energy." [10] However strange this coincidence between Vasconcelos and Professor Montague in metaphysics may sound on first hearing, it is intelligible in terms of the fact that both men are *neo*-Bergsonists. Where there is a common source, there is apt to be, other things being equal, a common outcome.)

How does Vasconcelos try to explain the passage from the lowest level of energy to its higher levels? The answer to this cosmological question does not appear until the last of the three antecedents to his system, *La revulsión de la energía* (1924), though it is suggested in mystical terms at the end of *El monismo estético.* The suggestion is that the passage from matter to superior modes of existence is governed by the law of the "regeneration" of energy. Art is energy spiritualized; its power is so great that it anticipates the "divine" state of energy.[11]

Just as Leibniz's *Monadology* may be regarded as his whole philosophy *in nuce,* so our author's twenty-page pamphlet on *The Revulsion of Energy* may be viewed as the recapitulation of his entire system of Aesthetic Monism. The essay is a magnificent *tour de force* in philosophy, containing all the separate strands of the system in miniature and drawing them together to form the unity developed in his subsequent writings. Its main thesis is that the cyclical hierarchy of existence known to man—matter, life, spirit—can only be explained by the theory of the "revulsion of energy." (The term "revulsion" is Vasconcelos' favorite name for the more familiar term "emergent" found in the literature of the contemporary movement called Emergent Evolution.)

Vasconcelos looks at himself as a revolutionist in cosmology, not as an evolutionist. He believes that more things are wrought by the alchemy of cosmic energy than Paracelsus ever dreamt of. Matter is mechanical energy; life, teleological energy; spirit, creative energy. Spirit is that mode of existence which is emancipated from all mundane concerns and works only for the greater glory of God. As life is energy demechanized, so spirit is energy deintellectualized; and that, according to the author, is the *aesthetic* way of life. It is unnecessary to go any further into the contents of *La revulsión de la energía* since its ideas are actually incorporated into the system five years later.[12]

IV. THE SYSTEM OF AESTHETIC MONISM

Aesthetic Monism as a system of philosophy rests on three interrelated postulates of beauty, all of which are derived from an admittedly mystical source. The three assumptions are as follows:[13]

(1) That beauty is a special form of cosmic energy.

(2) That the proper way of comprehending the nature of things is through aesthetic emotion.

(3) That the universe is not only running downwards but running upwards also, getting more and more beautiful.

Before considering Vasconcelos' arguments for these postulates, one should see how he relates his own contribution to the general history of philosophy. Granting that his system belongs to the Christian Neo-Platonic tradition, he claims, however, that it is "more thoroughgoing than any other version of Neo-Platonism,"[14] because it is grounded on the findings of contemporary science as well as on the insights of mysticism, old and new. In this connection, he interprets modern science as a "realism" in the nominalist sense and uses it to purify philosophic mysticism of all "abstractionism." But what he likes about science, it is important to distinguish, is its subject-matter, not its method. For the paradox of science, as he sees it, is that it deals with *concrete* things in an abstract way. Hence the methodological message of Aesthetic

Monism is, in brief, that we must go to art in order to meet this paradoxical situation. Science is not enough.[15]

The Vasconcelian system of philosophy is a trilogy. Its three parts, as originally conceived, are: *Tratado de metafísica* (1929), *Etica* (1932), and *Estética* (1936). As these volumes are actually members of a single body of ideas, they should be studied with the object of disengaging as much as possible the various arguments for the postulates listed at the head of this section.

A. The Case for Beauty as Energy

The first or metaphysical assumption of the Vasconcelian system, beauty as "aesthetic energy,"[16] is logically a derivative of the thesis that consciousness is an "invisible" form of energy, which in turn is a derivative of the thesis that reality as a whole is energy. This being the case, the first postulate of Aesthetic Monism is necessarily bound up with these two wider theses. Therefore, as the subsequent discussion will evince, arguments for the latter become by implication arguments for the former. After considerable digging into the *Treatise on Metaphysics,* I have managed to extract four possible arguments in support of the first postulate.

1. *The Existentialist Argument.* Vasconcelos starts off as a romanticist by attacking Cartesian rationalism and argues that existence is the necessary point of departure in matters philosophical. The immediate datum of my experience is "I am," not "I think." Hence *Sum* is ontologically prior to *Cogito.* Since I think because I exist and exist because I feel, consequently: I feel, therefore I exist. Vasconcelos erroneously believes that he is inverting the famous *Cogito ergo sum* of Descartes, but his own conclusion shows clearly that all he is really doing to it is restricting its general denotation to only the feeling-state of consciousness, that is, de-rationalizing it. At any rate, according to the *Treatise on Metaphysics,* to be is to be felt: *esse est sentiri.* Feeling is the criterion

of reality. Inasmuch as beauty is defined as a species of feeling, the inference is clear. Now feeling puts me in direct contact with other things besides myself. Hence the ultimate conclusion: I exist, therefore other things exist. What Santayana as a naturalist calls "animal faith" in the substantial world of events, Vasconcelos as a panpsychist calls *emoción.* The latter is even more existentialist than the former in that he has no realm of essence to distract him from the realm of existence. His is an "integral existentialism," as he has recently claimed out of desire to show his affinity to the most fashionable movement in present-day philosophy, not the "abstract existentialism," strange to say, he imputes to Martin Heidegger.[17]

The Vasconcelian system is nominalistic in the sense that it maintains that only particular "images" really exist. Accordingly, general "ideas" are nothing but the abstract and instrumental entities of reason. Now, since art deals with concretions in imagination, aesthetic experience is, therefore, at one with ultimate reality. And since all reality, ultimate or otherwise, is energy of some kind, *a fortiori* so is beauty. In the beginning was *Eros,* not *Logos.*[18]

The last three arguments of the author's metaphysics are written in the language of evolution, old and new. How far these arguments which follow are compatible with each other may be open to serious question.

2. *The Gradationalist Argument.* Borrowing a distinction from grammar, the Vasconcelian conception of the world contains only one common noun or substantive, namely, cosmic energy, the various manifestations of which constitute its manifold adjectives. Or to apply his own metaphor, the universe is like a cosmic symphony composed of variations on the same theme. Furthermore, these cosmic variations are to be interpreted in Leibnizian terms, *i.e.,* as differences of *degree;* in other words, they are not differences of *kind* (Descartes) nor of *aspect* (Spinoza). Thus

aesthetic energy is energy *sub gradu artis sive pulchritudinis.* This argument resolves the problem of monism versus pluralism by defending a diversified monism. Its logic is as deductive as it conclusion is seductive.[19]

3. *The Emanationist Argument.* The Vasconcelian system is a sort of "emanationism" in that it amends Plotinus with the Leibnizian concept of "fulguration," which is the ingenious alternative to both the theistic doctrine of creation and the pantheistic doctrine of emanation. In the beginning was God the Unknown, the creative energy whose "magical fluid" condenses, so to speak, into the heavens and the earth. Furthermore, this primal fluid proceeds out of its divine source in a certain pattern, in "triads," to be exact. The "dance of the Cosmos" is conceived after the analogy of a waltz, the three steps of which constitute the "cycles" of energy: physical, biological, psychical. The pattern of development, however, is not evolutionary in the modern scientific sense. Even though the higher cycles logically presuppose the lower, there is no more reason to suppose that the atom is at the beginning than at the end of the process of reality. Because the emanationist theory analyzes the general march of energy in logical and axiological terms, rather than in chronological ones, it follows that beauty must be one of its eternal emanations. This is evidently the most anti-Bergsonian of the author's arguments. His is no Gospel of Change: Vasconcelos is no modernist![20]

4. *The Emergentist Argument.* The hypothesis of "the revulsions of energy" serves as the "nerve" of Vasconcelos' whole speculation. The hypothesis defends a generalized phase rule to account for the changes from one cycle of energy to another, that is, the passage from atoms to cells and from these to souls. In other words, it extends the ice-water-steam situation in science to metaphysics, all of which points to a possible analogy between his theory of energy and the kinetic theory of gases.

The best way of understanding his thesis is to compare it with the contemporary movement of Emergent Evolution. Like Montague, Vasconcelos rightly complains that the school of Emergent Evolution simply states that there are unpredictable novelties or "emergents" in Nature and neatly describes what they are, but fails miserably to explain how these new factors come to be. On the other hand, the theory of "revulsions" holds that the appearance of novelties in the world is not surprising, but rather the necessary result of the general process of transformation characteristic of energy itself.[21]

So far it would seem that Vasconcelos is against that mood of accepting Nature which Samuel Alexander was fond of calling "natural piety." However, the same habit of mind appears in the system of Aesthetic Monism under the older and more austere name of destiny or the will of God. Now piety, whether natural or supernatural, is intellectual suicide. No thinker has the right to take his own life of reason by shirking the responsibility of trying to explain whatever mysteries permeate the world in which he lives and dies. To say, for example, that the structural ascent from a lower to a higher manifestation of energy is a "mysterious" *saltus* in Nature is to block the road to inquiry. After all, as Charles Peirce observed, it is precisely the "mysterious" itself which calls for an explanatory theory. To declare that the facts themselves, the "leaps" of energy in this case, are "mysterious" is to make them inexplicable by definition, thus defeating the very purpose of whatever hypothesis is proposed. It is, in fact, to miss the whole point of the function of hypothesis in the field of inquiry, which is to make as intelligible as possible what otherwise would remain a great mystery.

Despite the above limitation from which Vasconcelos suffers, he deserves credit at least for realizing more acutely than the emergent evolutionist that the different levels of Nature require some least common denominator in terms of which they are to be understood. Now, there are at least two reasons for his not going beyond this merely general requirement. First of all, he is not sufficiently acquainted with modern physics to exploit its distinction betwen kinetic and potential energy for metaphysical purposes, as Professor Montague has done with unusual clarity and originality in his Dewey paper, "A Materialistic Interpretation of Emergent Evolution," [22] published in the same year (1929) that the first volume of the Vasconcelian trilogy, *Tratado de metafísica,* appeared. It is a pity that, having had the germ of Montague's theory of mind as a form of potential energy when he first announced his system in 1918 and having gone so far as to suggest a sort of "wave" theory of thought in the *Treatise on Metaphysics,* he did not dèvelop this momentous hypothesis any further. The trouble, unfortunately, with Vasconcelos is that he has had too much piety as a mystic to be willing to go the new way of Montague, which is to explain spirit in physical terms without explaining away its psychical quality. And secondly, his spiritualistic interpretation of evolution adheres too much to Bergson to offer an adequate explanation of it even in the classic terms of emanation.

According to Vasconcelos, there are three distinct types of activity involved in the hierarchical "revulsions" of energy.[23] First, the atomic field of energy manifests itself as mechanical behavior. Atoms move hither and thither without growing up. Second, the vital field of energy is characterized instead by teleological action. Organisms operate with an eye on means and ends; they do not behave merely in terms of pushes and pulls. Third and last, the psychical field of energy is essentially aesthetic because the unique thing about souls is their creative work. More of this later. Suffice it to say at present that the "revulsionist" hypothesis is applied not only to the generic "revulsions" which energy undergoes in passing from one cycle to another, but is also applied to the specific "revulsions" within each cycle itself.

As with the most important example of the point just made, that of the psychical field of energy, the transition from one stage of consciousness to another is likewise explained as due to "revulsion." To Vasconcelos there are three "stages" (not "states") of consciousness. If defined in terms of their proper subject-matter, they are ideas, affects and images. Finally, from the preceding considerations it may be concluded that, in accordance with Aesthetic Monism, since consciousness as imagination is the highest form of psychical energy and since the latter is in turn the highest form of cosmic energy, *ergo* beauty, the product of imagination, is the highest form of reality. So much, then, for the arguments for the first postulate of the Vasconcelian system.

B. THE CASE FOR BEAUTY AS TRUTH

As a necessary preface to the discussion of the second or methodological assumption of Aesthetic Monism, beauty as truth, its epistemological presupposition should be examined first.

Vasconcelos uncritically accepts the doctrine of direct or monistic realism, which "assumes that the external world exists independently of the subject"[24] who apprehends it. Things exist even though we no longer experience them. The properties of external objects are independent of the knower, that is to say, they are not dependent on the mind for their existence, as the epistemological idealist or subjectivist claims. Moreover, in contrast to the position of the dualistic realist, the author believes that knowledge is an immediate apprehension of external things, not just a "copy" of them. To borrow Santayana's metaphors (so reminiscent of Spanish manners), the Mexican writer would say that truth is not only more than a "salute," but even more than an "embrace." It is, as he puts it, a "kiss" of love involving a mystical "identification of the soul with absolute being." While Santayana's "animal faith" issues only in an epistemological "salute"—a cold affair indeed—Vasconcelos has so much of that supernatural faith that removes mountains between the knowing subject and the object known that he interprets ultimate truth as the relation between a lover and his beloved.

The distinctive feature of Aesthetic Monism as a system of philosophy lies in its *aesthetic* methodology. Vasconcelos dares to preach the superiority of the method of the fine arts for acquiring knowledge at a time when the majority of experts teach and practise the method of the empirical sciences. He not only retains with Croce the basic thesis that art has a cognitive function, but goes so far as to insist with Schelling and Schopenhauer that aesthetic experience gives us knowledge of reality. Whereas that Italian neo-Hegelian, in fact, defines art as *pre*-conceptual knowledge, the Mexican neo-Bergsonist defines it as *post*-conceptual knowledge. Thus his message is even more radical than Croce's, because it actually identifies art with logic itself; Croce and almost everybody else keep them distinct. Imagination ("artistic emotion") is hailed as the *novum organum.*[25]

Viewed historically, this bold defense of art for *logic's* sake takes us back to Schelling's conviction that art is the *organon* of philosophy. The Vasconcelian position is essentially a romanticized version of Schelling's vision of art *minus* its Platonizing background. Strange as it may sound, although credit is given to Schelling for the richness of his "extraordinary conjectures,"[26] including the "hierarchical scale" of Truth, Goodness and Beauty, no connection is ever made by Vasconcelos between the intuitions of that German romanticist and his own view. One reason for this absence of comparison is that his knowledge of Schelling's transcendental philosophy is indirect, his source of information being restricted apparently to the historical allusions found in Croce's *Estetica*.

Vasconcelos tells us that his theory of knowledge is the *modus operandi* of his general doctrine of the "revulsions" of cosmic energy. Inasmuch as each cycle or order of reality "possesses its own logic" appropriate to it and inasmuch as there are three cycles of reality—the physical, the biological, and the psychical—it follows that the Vasconcelian system has a "trinitarian" logic.[27]

The three organs of knowledge are named after the tripartite division of the old faculty psychology: intellect, will, feeling. Accordingly, the intellect is the method appropriate to the study of matter; the will, the method appropriate to the study of life; feeling, the method appropriate to the study of consciousness. In other words, methodologically speaking, Vasconcelos is an intellectualist in physics, a voluntarist in biology and an intuitionist in psychology. All of which signifies that he attempts to solve the methodological problem by indicating in a neat but artificial fashion what he considers the appropriate domain for each of the three assumed ways of knowing. That is to say, he holds that different subject-matters call for different methods of knowing. (Of the three proposed ways of knowing, the most ambiguous member of the logical trinity is the so-called "voluntary method" of the will. It is not clear whether will and intelligence operate alike; what is clear, to be sure, is the desire to keep the trinitarian pattern at any cost.)

Scientific method is defined in the Bergsonian sense, *i.e.,* as the analytic operation of intelligence. Its proper subject-matter is physical things, the first order of reality. Therefore a scientific physics is possible, but a scientific metaphysics is not. Instead of saying to all this, as one would expect, so much the worse for metaphysics, Vasconcelos reacts the other way around. For Aesthetic Monism "implies a hierarchy of knowing" which corresponds to "the scale of existence." A higher degree of reality goes together with a higher degree of knowledge. Hence emotion, through which we have access to a "synthesis of noumena," is superior to intellect, through whose means we can arrive at only a "synthesis of phenomena." [28]

Although Vasconcelos is justified, given the assumption of his hierarchical system, in arguing for the superiority of "the emotional method" over the method of science, he is not justified in stating that argument in the above terms, because the distinction made between the two syntheses implies that via intellect the human mind deals with appearances alone and thus not with reality itself. This implication is inconsistent with the system's premise that the intellect is the way of knowing the first order of reality. After all, a conception of degrees of reality permits the more or less real, but never the non-real (or apparent). Vasconcelos has such little faith in intelligence, not to say reason, that he makes a worse case for it than he should within his own system.

The recent volume on *Organic Logic* (1945) discusses methodology in terms of the beloved word "coordination" instead of the earlier term "synthesis." There are two kinds of *coordinación,* namely, "coordination of the homogeneous" and "coordination of the heterogeneous." [29] These define, respectively, the two limits of human knowledge: the abstract pole of mathematics and the concrete pole of music. Knowledge "advances" from the greatest homogeneity to the greatest heterogeneity (a methodological echo of Spencerian evolution plus Schopenhauerian aesthetics). Mathematic, the deductive science *par excellence,* coordinates the homogeneous by reducing the qualitative wholes or the variety of things to quantitative parts or units *all alike.* Physics, being an experimental science, is "more than mathematics." Its data are sensory, not purely formal; and its methods are inductive, rather than deductive. The mathematical form that its generalizations take is due to the relative homogeneity of matter itself. Physics deals with repeatable events whose behavior is predominantly mechanical in character. As the heterogeneity of the data investigated *increases,* the mathematical possibility of interpreting them *decreases.* Because natural science, by hypothesis, cannot in fact coordinate either the homogeneous or the heterogeneous, one may say for the author that its work is to subordinate the heterogeneous to the homogeneous for the sake of utility. Its function, in brief, is instrumental. Thus Vasconcelos, after his master Bergson, "pragmatizes" positive science in order to deny its validity as an ultimate way of knowing.

By "organic logic" is meant the type of thinking that coordinates "heterogeneities" or "wholes." (Note the unacknowledged influence of the Gestalt school of psychology: "organic" thinking is perception of "wholes.") Since it is identified with the "third order of knowing," whose subject-matter is consciousness, he should have called it *superorganic* logic in order to avoid its possible confusion with the second order of knowing, which deals with living beings or organisms. The title *Organic Logic* is deliberately given to the book as a tribute to Whitehead, but the tribute seems to be misplaced. At any rate, its central thesis is that genuine thinking is "organic" in character. To think concretely is "to coordinate wholes," not reduce the particular to the general, as all scientific generalizations do.

If science as abstract thought conceives the world in terms of "formal" universals, what operation of human consciousness perceives it in terms of "concrete" universals? The answer to this question goes straight to the heart of the Vasconcelian system. Here it is in one phrase: "aesthetic emotion." The concrete universal is the *aesthetic* universal, the essence of which lies in "its power of harmonizing heterogeneities and giving them meaning." [30] Hence the *Logos Artístico* is the Word made flesh.

Consciousness in its aesthetic phase is, according to Vasconcelos, concrete thinking. Whereas science decomposes, art recomposes. The "aesthetic syllogism" handles concrete "images" rather than abstract "ideas." As the model of scientific knowledge is mathematics, so the model of artistic knowledge is music. Mathematical logic involves a "falsification" of reality; only a logic based on imagination, the mind's "synthesizing" faculty *par excellence,* can put us in rapport with the divine scheme of things entire. Hence the system of Aesthetic Monism gets its name from the unity-in-variety intrinsic to music as against the uniformity typical of mathematics. Vasconcelos is, to adopt the phrase he applied over thirty years ago to Pythagoras of old, "Pythagoras the aesthete" in new dress.[31]

As the "revulsionist" hypothesis is the nerve of Vasconcelos' cosmology, so one may state that his conception of "the aesthetic *a priori*"[32] is the nerve of his methodology, to which he has quite recently attached the name of "the philosophy of coordination."[33] The thesis of the *Apriori Estético,* submitted to make intelligible the "organic nature" of creative thought,[34]

> ... consists in maintaining that just as the mind has categories of space-time, of genus and species, it is also endowed with special forms of understanding applicable to the aesthetic phenomenon, forms which clarify beauty, and these forms are rhythm, melody, and harmony.

Irrespective of the technical objections to this passage that any student acquainted with Kantian terminology could easily raise, it is clear that Vasconcelos is trying to have his "aesthetic trinity" of rhythm, melody, and harmony do for *artistic* perception (in the sense of "organic" truth) what Kant's "pure forms" of space and time do for *ordinary* perception. However, no proof whatsoever is presented in support of such an aesthetic trascendentalism, which, incidentally, reminds one of Scheler's "emotional *a priori*." Vasconcelos is no Kant! For his whole conception of the "organic" nature of thought is based simply on an analogy with counterpoint in music. Organic thinking is identified with aesthetic thinking. To think artistically, that is, to "coordinate" the multiple "zones of reality," each of which is subject to its own laws—from the molecular to the spiritual—is as different from the supposedly reductive nature of scientific thought as, he illustrates, a Bach theme with variations differs from a sorites in syllogistic reasoning.[35] The difference, in brief, is one between a *concrete* logic of art and an *abstract* logic of science. It is of course only the former that is faithful to the "holistic" (Jan Smuts) pattern of reality.

In the volume on *Aesthetics,* Vasconcelos regards his hypothesis of the *Apriori Estético* as "in large part" his own discovery and his one contribution at least to the field of philosophy. He made the same claim in a paper before the Second Inter-American Congress of Philosophy held in 1947 at Columbia University.[36] If one asks wherein lies the originality of his aesthetic transcendentalism, a comparison with Croce and Bergson may yield the answer. For in all probability the phrase "aesthetic *a priori*" was consciously or unconsciously taken over from Croce's *Breviario di estetica* (1913), a Spanish edition of which appeared in Mexico City in 1925. The meaning, however, given to that Crocian phrase, whose origin is doubtless Kantian, must have come from Bergson's *Le Rire* (1900; English trans., 1911).

To support this guess, here are the key passages from the Spanish edition of the *Breviario di estetica* and the English edition of the classic on *Laughter*: "Art is a true *aesthetic a priori* synthesis of feeling and image within intuition" (Croce); "Art is certainly only a more direct vision of reality" (Bergson).[37] Should these two statements be joined to form a metaphysic of art, the net product would be precisely the author's "method of aesthetics" as *the* way of knowing the nature of things: *the* logic of logics. In contrast to Croce, who insists on distinguishing between art and philosophy as species of knowledge, the former being "alogical" or "pre-logical," Vasconcelos arrives at a mystic union of the two. If Croce's doctrine of intuition as the key to aesthetics is married to Bergson's doctrine of intuition as the key to metaphysics, the result would be the Vasconcelian doctrine of intuition as the key to logic. Thus Croce and Vasconcelos would agree generically as to the cognitive significance of art, but would disagree with respect to its specific kind of knowledge. The two thinkers are diametrically opposed on the latter issue because, to repeat, the Italian conceives art as *pre*-conceptual, the Mexican as *post*-conceptual.

The implication of the view of art as post-conceptual knowledge is *logical dualism,* that is, the belief in a higher or absolute logic as contra-distinguished from a lower or relative one. The greatest irony of Asthetic Monism is that it leads to a logical dualism: Art versus Science. Besides, it should be obvious from the foregoing that the method of intuition or "emotion" (Vasconcelos prefers the latter "weasel" word to the former) can be manipulated by the philosopher to form the queerest of unions. Yet, in any case, whether the child born of the Croce-Bergson marriage in Mexico is legitimate or not, the fact still remains that it constitutes Vasconcelos' "baby." Like every new baby, it has at least the property of being different, and anything having that property in the realm of philosophy is worthy of attention. This does not mean, of course, that originality of thought is more important in philosophy than the attainment of truth.

It should also be obvious from the above considerations that Vasconcelos has more affinity to Bergson than to Croce. Nevertheless, in spite of their common appeal to intuition and their common aversion to science, there is a rather significant difference between Bergson and Vasconcelos, which justifies calling the latter a neo-Bergsonist. That difference lies in the fact that the Mexican has made explicit what is but implicit in the Frenchman's eloquent plea for metaphysics as against positive science, to wit, that metaphysics can truly substantiate its claim to dispense with the abstract concepts of science if and only if it operates with the concrete intuitions of the artist. For inasmuch as the artist is defined as the logician *par excellence,* it follows that the "aesthetic criterion," which, by hypothesis, consists in coordinating smaller wholes *all different* into larger ones, is closer to "living reality" than the analytic criterion of the scientist. In short, while Bergson tried to tell the contemporary world what is wrong with science, Vasconcelos has aimed at telling it what is right with art. The latter's message is doubtless the other (positive) side of the former's.

This leads us to what is perhaps the most ironical thing about Bergson's well-known doctrine of intuition (not to be confused with Croce's quite different view, that intuition apprehends "possible" objects rather than "real" ones). Despite the fact that the general position of the Paris philosopher may be denominated a "Panaestheticism" written in biological terms, he never really set himself to working out in any detail a theory of art. The irony, to be sure, is to a great extent understandable on the ground that a Panaestheticism talks so much about the aesthetic in general that it requires no separate theory of aesthetics in particular. Be that as it may, the closest Bergson ever came to formulating a philosophy of art is to be found in the middle part of the last chapter of his small volume on *Laughter,* which has already been mentioned. That part claims to do no more than sketch its "main outlines." But fortunately for Vasconcelos, Bergson the master left his Mexican disciple something to complete. For the method of Aesthetic Monism is essentially an expansion and a clarification of the Bergsonian thesis that art brings us "face to face with reality itself." Connecting this thesis with its intuitionist companion in *An Introduction to Metaphysics* (1903), one arrives at Vasconcelos' bold identification of aesthetics with metaphysics. That the disciple is not altogether conscious of what he has done to his master is somewhat irrelevant. What is relevant, after all, is that he carries out the Bergsonian premise in *Le Rire* to its ultimate end. For if art brings us "face to face with reality itself," then it follows that metaphysical truth is *artistic* truth.

Though Bergson originally gave art a supreme cognitive status in his essay on *Laughter* in 1900, his subsequent writings have had the effect of lowering its truth-value. Not that he loves art less, but he loves philosophy more. The different arts still provide "a much more direct vision of reality" than the natural sciences "because the artist is less intent on utilizing his perception" than the ordinary man. Yet philosophy can "lead us to a completer perception of reality" and its satisfactions are "more frequent, more continual and more accessible to the majority of men" than those we receive from art.[38] In fact, a case could easily be made from *An Introduction to Metaphysics* that the French philosopher puts philosophy above art on the ground that philosophic intuition dispenses with the sensory images of artistic intuition and, accordingly, has a deeper insight into reality. This being so, it follows that the closest parallel in the history of Western philosophy to the Vasconcelian doctrine concerning the logical import of *aesthetic* emotion is, again, Schelling's suggestion in the *System des transcendentalen Idealismus,* that art is the *organon* of philosophy. What is only a pregnant guess, however, in that romantic idealist, turns out to be the key to a whole system of philosophy in Vasconcelos.

To summarize the arguments for the second postulate of the system of Aesthetic Monism—art as truth—one may infer that metaphysics must use the "aesthetic method" on a grand scale in order to reach its goal of a unitary vision of the world. In other words, the only way of knowing ultimate reality is by artistic intuition. Hence, the proper field of philosophy is aesthetics, conceived as the specific logic of beauty. And since metaphysical truth, by hypothesis, is artistic truth, it follows that beauty constitutes the highest form of truth.

For an understanding and appreciation of this view of what philosophy is or ought to be, a comparison with what Russell used to think (before the publication of his *Human Knowledge* in 1948) may help. To both the earlier Russell and Vasconcelos, philosophy is logic. The former, however, used to conceive philosophy after the analogy of mathematics; in contrast, the latter views it in terms of music. Now, one must frankly admit that there is something novel and appealing in the Mexican author's *aesthetic* interpretation of philosophy, especially in the light of the fact that most conceptions about the nature of philosophy either relegate the artistic side of experience to a secondary post or neglect it altogether. Nevertheless, if Vasconcelos is right, artists are by nature philosophers and, should this be the case, why so much ado about asking philosophers to become artists? His unique faith in nothing but the "aesthetic method" is analogous to the more common faith among our contemporary thinkers in nothing but the "scientific method." Both faiths tend to reduce philosophy to something other than what it really is. Besides, to comment in passing on Vasconcelos' brand of faith in beauty as *the Truth*, whether the way of art is cognitively superior to the way of science and whether it is in fact a way of knowing at all—these two matters are, of course, debatable questions into which it is out of place to enter in this book.

The final or axiological postulate of Vasconcelos' system of philosophy, the third assumption of ascending spirit, is really a consequence of the other two. To expose the nerve of his whole argument for beauty as value, all one needs do is to translate the relatively descriptive language of the foregoing discussion into normative terms. If this is done, the result is what he calls "hierarchical monism." [39] or to use that favorite metaphor of his again, a "spiral" conception of the universe. The universe is envisaged as running upwards and its "geometry of becoming" may be figuratively described as a "winding staircase." For, according to his point of view, the "trinitarian order" accessible to theory of reality has to be the "same order" accessible to theory of value. That is, the realm of existence is coextensive with the realm of value, so much so that even the poor atom of physics ceases to be mere *res extensa* and becomes *res significans*. Thus consciousness as spirit is the seat of values, without which the universe would have no rhyme or reason.

To show Vasconcelos' scale of values by way of contrast, one may say that "the aesthetic method" makes the world not only a thing of knowledge but, at the same time, a thing of beauty. Hence the realm of value is also coextensive with the realm of knowledge: value = knowledge = reality. All of which signifies that the aesthetic quality of spiritual experience is accorded a higher value than its ethical quality. Whereas the Kantian system of philosophy, to cite the most obvious example in the history of Western thought, assigns the primacy to "practical reason," Vasconcelos subscribes instead to the primacy of "aesthetic judgment." To him the sense of beauty is superior to the sense of duty.

Aesthetic Monism maintains that consciousness has two aspects —the theoretical and the practical—each of which contains three stages of development. *Sub specie cognitionis,* these stages are: the intellectual, the volitional and the emotional. *Sub specie valoris,* they are, respectively, as follows: the scientific, the ethical and the aesthetic. In addition to the belief that the three ascending orders of reality—the physical, the biological and the psychical—have their appropriate method of inquiry, Vasconcelos believes that each of them possesses its characteristic value. Science is the value accessible to matter; morals, the value accessible to life; art, the value accessible to spirit. Consequently it is in art that spirit seeks its own level. All of these culminate in religion, the ultimate in value. Here, then, is the Vasconcelian scale of values *in nuce.* At this point, a quick review of its several modes is in order.[40]

To begin with science, his attitude towards its value is completely Bergsonian. Despite the frequent claim that his system is rooted in the teachings of contemporary science, the general direction of his thought is essentially one of disparagement of its methods. The only value he really concedes to its conceptual operations is practical or economic in the Machian sense. In other words, science to him is knowledge for power, action, adaptation to environment: a purely biological affair. To restrict, however, both the scope of the scientific method to 'a "lower" order of reality and its function to technology, as he does, is to make science the handmaid of a preconceived system of philosophy. It is to prejudge unduly its powers and limits in theory as well as in practice. Vasconcelos "pragmatizes" science so much that he fails to understand and appreciate the self-corrective character of its techniques. As to the significance itself of this Bergsonian approach to natural science, it is chiefly negative, *i.e.,* it reminds us that science is not the only way in the pursuit of wisdom.

The second stage of spiritual activity, moral conduct, is characterized by "teleological action" as against the mechanical behavior of physical bodies. Since purposive activity goes with the "anti-entropic" nature of all living things, the moral life is life on the biological plane raised to the status of value. Its value, like science's, is nevertheless instrumental, not intrinsic. And contrary to what one might have expected from his hierarchical conception of Nature, Vasconcelos makes the cute suggestion that a "botanical norm" is superior to a "zoological" one.[41] To him, plants live on a higher level than animals. A "botanical ethics" would be more humane than the "Jungle" ethics envisioned by Kipling and taken seriously by the tough Darwinians. Man, the author warns, will really "go to the dogs" if he doesn't learn how to live like plants.

The general thesis [42] of the *Ethics,* the second volume of the trilogy, is negatively stated in the following way: the standard of conduct can neither be determined by a formal nor by a utilitarian formula. That is to say, both Immanuel Kant and John Stuart Mill are wrong in ethical theory. As to a free or sanctionless morality *à la* Russell or Montague, the Mexican author is of the opinion that such a view is meaningless. On the contrary, he believes that moral values must be subordinated first to "aesthetic ends" and these in turn, to the "superhuman ends" of religion. Although all this is obviously orthodox enough in making religion the ultimate sanction of right conduct, its heterodox element lies in the fact that art is made its proximate criterion. To the religious authoritarian, art covers a multitude of sins, but to Vasconcelos it is or ought to be both the foundation of morals and the preface to religion. The political implication of Aesthetic Monism is, therefore, that the City of God will not come to pass until *artists* become kings.

The most popular and, at the same time, the most fantastic side of Vasconcelos' thought is to be found in his social ideas. The *Ethics* ends with a Politics writ small, the chief sources of which are two companion volumes, *La raza cósmica* (1925) and *Indología* (1927), together with *Bolivarismo y monroísmo* (1935).[43] Their theme is Ibero-Americanism (the Bolívar Doctrine) versus Anglo-Americanism (the Monroe Doctrine). They were written during the period when the Mexican "Ulysses" was editor of *La Antorcha* and a politician extremely sensitive to so-called "Yankee imperialism." In all fairness, it should be added that since the Good Neighbor Policy of the United States has gone into effect, he has become more sympathetic to Anglo-American values. His recent lecture tour in the United States under the auspices of the Rockefeller Foundation is evidence of his change of heart. As a matter of fact, even when he was a militant critic of *el imperialismo yanqui,* he declared in a lecture under the Harris Foundation at the University of Chicago in 1926:[44]

> The fact that this continent is divided among Anglo-Saxons and Latins should be looked upon then as a blessing; because we all long for a higher, richer spiritual world, and it is only through the work of singularly gifted groups of people that a true all-comprehending type of civilization may come to life. The bigoted patriot who may dream of an all-Yankee America extending its shops from Patagonia to Canada is just as potent a foe to the true ends of mankind as the blind Latin-American chauvinist who may dream of a time of decay in which the Yankee standards of life are to be substituted by the newer southern manners of life. The one comforting fact is that differences of temperament and of soul tend to create sympathy and friendliness rather than opposition and scorn, and this should be borne in mind whenever any conflict of a material character may arise among our nations.

Nevertheless, despite his plea for continental unity-in-variety, it is the anti-Yankee phase of his thought which originally made him stand out in all of Latin America as the loudspeaker of his "race." The very seal of the National University of Mexico bears the racialist strain of Vasconcelism: *Por mi raza hablará el espiritu.*

There are two components to Vasconcelos' social philosophy, a speculative anthropology and a still more speculative history. With respect to the first, he predicts that a "cosmic race" will emerge to fulfil "the divine mission of America." This *raza cósmica* will represent the "synthesis" of the four races now existing —the black, the brown, the yellow, and the white. Each member of the new stock will be a *Totinem,* a "whole man." Now, since he contends that North America acts on the anti-human and anti-Christian principle of racial segregation and, *per contra,* that Latin America acts on the opposite principle of *mestizaje,* he concludes consequently that the germ of the "cosmic race" of the future is to be found in the present peoples living below the Rio Grande. Vasconcelos introduces some speculative geography for good measure and puts his faith in the tropics around the Amazon region. Whatever one may think of him as a prophet of a "cosmic race" in tropical America, he is ingenious enough to imagine its possibility in a universe of "cosmic energy."

As to what that "divine mission of America" is, one must go to his theory of human history for the answer. Like Comte, he believes that society passes through three stages of culture, but he defines them in keeping with his own system as follows: the material, the political and the aesthetic. On the basis of this statement of social development, it is clear that the mission of the New World is to bring about what Friedrich Schiller called an "aesthetic state." Inasmuch as such a society can only be realized by an "emotional race" having a sense of beauty and inasmuch as this gift is possessed "to a high degree" by the hybrid peoples of Latin America, it follows that their responsibility, as well as their privilege, lies in working towards its realization. But, in order to achieve their mission, they must get rid of the "gross pragmatism" that has, alas, corrupted them even more than North Americans, the strength of whom derives from their Puritan tradition. This note of warning shows that Vasconcelos, like many a father, chastises those whom he loves. For though he sides with Latin Americans ethnically, he attacks them ethically for their corrupt ways of living. No matter how utopian or quixotic the Mexican "Ulysses" may sound on many an occasion, he is sufficiently practical at times, after all, to get down to earth.

As a corollary of his *aesthetic* interpretation of history, he thinks it behooves an "emotional race" such as his to develop a philosophy based on "the particular logic of the emotions and beauty." Hundreds of philosophies in the past have been constructed with the data of the senses and the rules of reason, but the philosophies of the future, so he predicts at the end of his *History of Philosophic Thought,* will be aesthetic in character.[45] The principal reason for his forecast—doubtless a keen observation on his part—is that the field of aesthetics provides a real possibility of bridging the gap between facts and values, the *crux philosophorum.* For every aesthetic fact, say a melody, is *res significans* as well as *factum.* Art, in other words, actually harmonizes the real and the ideal. In contrast to the usual status of morals in human experience, the artist practises more or less what he preaches. Incidentally, since Vasconcelos believes that aesthetic philosophy is the style of thinking most congenial to the "Hispanic temperament," he also predicts that the philosophy of the future will be in the hands of the "emotional race" to which he belongs.

This leads naturally to the aesthetic phase of spirit. Before taking up its nature, however, there are one or two comments which need to be made in passing. In the first place, given Aesthetic Monism as a general philosophy, it is really impossible to disengage its "aesthetic theory of the world" from aesthetics proper as a special branch of philosophical inquiry. For experience gets so "aestheticized" in such a system that it is hard to tell what its specific aesthetic aspect is. Vasconcelos is the best or the worst example (depending on one's point of view) of a man who writes about art in terms of a preferred system of philosophy, rather than in its own language. So much so that he describes his philosophic position as a "metaphysic of aesthetics." [46] There is a vast difference between that kind of thing and a philosophy of art that attempts to understand the artistic aspect of human experience as such. The difference, sharply put, is one between theorizing about *aesthetics* and theorizing about *art*. The first, what Vasconcelos does *ad nauseam*, theorizes about something itself theoretical; *per contra,* the other theorizes about something not actually theoretical in itself, though potentially so or at least accessible to understanding. Moreover, the fact that he makes no serious effort to distinguish the two terms, "art" and "beauty," his emphasis falling on the latter, gives his doctrine away as an "aesthetic metaphysics" or an "aesthetic logic." Had he, on the other hand, held to his implicit adjectival analysis of art, the purpose of which is to extend its domain beyond what Dewey has fitly called "the museum conception of art," [47] he would have analyzed "the aesthetic" as a specific quality of all possible experience without confounding it with "aesthetics," the theoretical discipline whose aim is to determine the nature of that quality.

Vasconcelos' conception of beauty as the highest species of knowledge points to what he has to say about beauty as the highest species of value. In contrast to the analytic operations of the intellect and the teleological conduct of the will, the aesthetic stage of mind, or "aesthetic energy," to translate back into the language of cosmology, is characterized by "creative activity." Because of its creative quality, beauty is a higher value than intelligence and character. In fact, the author goes so far as to identify the "aesthetic order" with St. Augustine's (and Pascal's) *ordo amoris.* It seems that artists to him are the closest thing to angels! What is beauty, then? As content, it is "emotion *sui generis*"; as form, it is "successful composition." Though beauty is non-teleological, it is *not* disinterested. The latter is too neutral a predicate for Vasconcelos. The artist, as he finally sees him, is ultimately interested in saving his own soul via his work. Hence art is not "disinterested pleasure," as it is for Kant, Bergson and Caso; one may formulate his definition of art as "interested creation." By "creation," however, is meant coordination of heterogeneous materials already given, not something *ex nihilo.* Thus creation is really *re*-creation. This last implication is not actually drawn by the author. It follows nevertheless from his fundamental category of coordination.

Since art mediates the chasm between the ideal and the real, Vasconcelos ultimately identifies the theoretical aspect of aesthetic experience with its practical aspect, beauty as knowledge with beauty as value. As a consequence, he would not agree, say, with Santayana, who distinguishes between beauty as value and truth as fact. To adapt Keat's famous lines to his view, beauty is "organic" truth and "organic" truth is beauty, but that is *not* all ye need to know on earth. There is one more thing beyond beauty ye still need to know. Some call it religion; others call it God. Thus Vasconcelos' philosophical Ode to Beauty is the prelude to his Hymn to God.

At long last, the final destination of the Odyssey of the Mexican "Ulysses" is in sight. From beginning to end there is God in his aesthetic vision of the universe. To be sure, his God is not a cosmic Mathematician, like Jeans'; he is, rather, a cosmic Musician. The Vasconcelian Gospel preaches Big Beauty, not Big Business. All roads lead to God, but the God they lead to is neither the impersonal Force of the pantheist nor the abstract Idea of the panlogist. In contrast, to borrow a term from James Mark Baldwin, one might call Vasconcelos a "pancalist" (from the Greek *pan* and *kalos*) on the ground that the whole universe to him is a thing of beauty which anticipates a joy for ever. To avoid both pantheism, the "natural danger" [48] of a monistic philosophy, and panlogism, its artificial danger, all one must do, according to Vasconcelos, is to state their first principles in reverse. Thus, personality or spirit in the concrete becomes elevated to the basic and ultimate nature of the world, thereby making possible the inference to the personal God of Christian faith. Incidentally, this belief in a Supreme Person, "the Whole of wholes," discloses that strain of Vasconcelos' thought which has led him to ally himself in the last few years with the movement of North American Personalism, especially as represented by Professor E. S. Brightman of Boston University.

Just as the Mexican writer holds that morality at its best is aesthetic in character, that is, action from sympathy rather than from duty, so he maintains that the "highest grade" of aesthetic experience itself is "religious feeling."[49] The cup of beauty, so to speak, runneth over into religion. Thus beauty is the highest form of value because the mystic stage of art is one with religious experience; and conversely, religion is ultimate beauty.

A final word or two about his theology, containing still an unresolved mixture of mysticism and authoritarianism. Succinctly put, his creed sounds more or less like this: religion is the highest embodiment of feeling; revelation, the highest form of knowledge; liturgy, the supreme point of the arts; St. Francis of Assisi, the best of saints; the Roman Catholic, the "most perfect" of churches known to man. The volume on *Aesthetics* terminates with a promise of a forthcoming work on Theodicy, which may reconcile the mystical and authoritarian strands of his philosophy of religion. In this connection, I understand from the author himself that he is at the moment preparing a volume which is to be the consummation of his trilogy—*Metafísica, Etica, Estética.* Its title is probably going to be *Mística.* Of course, whether the Roman Catholic Church or, for that matter, any church, will look with favor upon the confessions of an aesthetic mystic, is rather doubtful. Be that as it may, the evident implication of Aesthetic Monism is *religious* monism, which is Bergson's "complete mysticism." But to repeat what was said near the beginning of the chapter, whereas Bergson felt somewhat ashamed of the mysticism to which his findings led him, Vasconcelos on the other hand is perhaps our only *unashamed* mystic in Western philosophy living today.

The Vasconcelian system of philosophy, then, is a "diversified monism" in cosmology, an "aesthetic monism" in methodology and an "hierarchical monism" in axiology.

5

Perspectivism and
Existentialism in Mexico

I. ORTEGA IN MEXICO

The first decade of the twentieth century in Mexico was a time of ferment in politics and of rebellion in philosophy. Chapter II attempted to show that the revolt against positivism, the official philosophy of the Porfirist régime, was given public expression in the final lecture delivered by Vasconcelos under the auspices of the Ateneo de la Juventud in 1910. Likewise, though not to the same degree, the third decade of the present century was a period of rebellion in Mexican philosophy, this time, however, against the Bergsonizing orientation of the Generation of the Centennial. What was the keynote of the new rebellion and who were the first insurgents?

To quote from the recent account by Samuel Ramos, the initiator of the revolt:[1]

> An intellectual generation which began to act publicly between 1925 and 1930 felt dissatisfied with the philosophical romanticism of Caso and Vasconcelos. After a critical revision of their doctrines, they found

anti-intellectualism groundless, but they did not wish to return to class-ical rationalism. In this perplexity, the books of José Ortega y Gasset began to arrive in Mexico, and in the first of them, *Meditaciones del Quijote,* they encountered the solution to the conflict in his doctrine of *vital reason.* In addition, as a result of the revolution, a spiritual change had been going on, which, starting around 1915, was becoming clarified in the minds of people and could be defined in these terms: Mexico had been discovered. It was a nationalist movement which was being extended little by little to Mexican culture: in poetry with Ramón López Velarde, in painting with Diego Rivera, in the novel with Mari-ano Azuela. Vasconcelos himself, from the Ministry of Education, had been talking of forming a national culture and was promoting all efforts in that direction. Meanwhile philosophy did not appear to fit within this ideal picture of nationalism because she has always pre-tended to look at things from the standpoint of man in general; hence, opposed to the concrete determinations of space and time, that is to say, to history. Ortega y Gasset came also to solve this problem by showing the historicity of philosophy in his *El tema de nuestro tiempo.* Assem-bling these ideas with some others he had expounded in *Meditaciones del Quijote,* that Mexican generation found the epistemological justification of a national philosophy.

The Mexican generation of which Ramos speaks is his own, usually referred to as the Generation of Contemporáneos. This generation gets its name from a very small group of *literatos,* who, imbued with a feeling of spiritual restlessness and a sense for the problematic character of human life, organized in 1928 a society called "Contemporáneos" and published a journal under the same title. The literary group consisted of seven friends, nick-named "the seven wise men of Mexico." The official philosopher of Contemporáneos was Samuel Ramos himself and its unofficial one was José Romano Muñoz. The latter is reported to have been the first to import Ortega's ideas from Madrid and circulate them throughout Mexico.

Both Ramos and Romano had beeen Caso's students at the National University of Mexico and, originally, ardent admirers of his. Of the two men, however, Ramos was the rebel who dared in 1927 to reverse his opinion about the value of Caso as a philosopher and launched a one-man campaign in the first three issues of *Ulises* (the predecessor of *Contemporáneos*) against his teacher's "anti-intellectualism" and its primary source, Bergson's intuitionism. (Ramos was too sympathetic with Vasconcelos' nationalist policy in education to attack his *romanticismo filosófico* at the time.) In contrast to the rebellious Ramos, Romano was more the peacemaker and compromiser. This can be easily gathered from his October, 1927, article in the fourth number of *Ulises*: "Neither Irrationalism nor Rationalism, but Critical Philosophy." By this he does not mean Kant's philosophy, but a compromise solution to the perennial conflict between reason and intuition. Accordingly, the true philosophic method is one in which these two ways of knowing complement each other. Although the author does not explicitly state that the solution he proposes to the above antinomy is virtually the same as Ortega's theory of *la razón vital,* he is honest enough to admit that Caso had foreseen the method appropriate to philosophy in the *Problemas filosóficos,* published in 1915. Nevertheless, he agrees entirely with Ramos that their teacher had "godfathered" intuition so much as to have produced an enervating effect on the Mexicans, a "lazy and irresolute" people who need, as Ortega himself had warned, precision in thinking more than anything else for intellectual development. The article closes with the flat assertion that Bergson is no longer in fashion and urges the Mexican people to rejuvenate themselves with the new and fertile ideas coming out of Germany and Italy, as well as those from North and South America.[2]

In spite of the above request of the elder member of Contemporáneos that his countrymen go beyond Bergson and learn the new ways of philosophy not only in Germany but in other lands as well, subsequent events conclusively show that the influence of Ortega as Germanophile was so great in Mexico that, with a few exceptions, the majority of the contemporary philosophers read by Mexican students have been the very same ones to whom that Spanish thinker gave his editorial blessings a generation or so ago. The lucky ones by and large were those associated with the phenomenological movement. The reasons for Ortega's Germanic bias, so manifest in his very first volume, *Meditaciones del Quijote* (1914), cannot be discussed here because they would involve a long digression on the tribulations of the contemporary Spanish soul, together with the trials of the Generation of '98 to straighten out "invertebrate Spain." It is sufficient to say that the principal factor responsible for the introduction of contemporary German philosophy into Latin America is precisely Ortega's editorial work both as publisher-editor of the internationally known *Revista de Occidente,* which he founded in 1922, and as director of the large publishing house in Madrid, Espasa-Calpe.

Of all the philosophical currents in twentieth-century Germany, it is the existentialist wing of the phenomenological movement that has become the most fashionable way of thinking in the academic circles of Latin America, particularly in Mexico. The career of phenomenology proper below the Rio Grande has been rather sporadic. Edmund Husserl, the essence-intoxicated man, was too much of a pure logician for the Latin-American mind. Like the Stagirite of old, Latin Americans as a rule yearn to bring the realm of essence down to earth. Thus, however strange it may sound to some, Martin Heidegger is much more appealing to them than the late philosopher from Freiburg.

In regard to the other factors that have contributed to what may be called the "Germanization" of the Mexican mind in recent years, mention should first be made that when Ortega's editorial activities were interrupted by the Spanish Civil War in 1936, various publishing houses in Latin America, especially Fondo de Cultura Económica in Mexico City and Editorial Losada in Buenos Aires, took upon themselves the task of continuing his far-reaching project of making German philosophical literature available in Spanish. In the second place, several Mexican scholars went directly to Germany to study philosophy around the late 'twenties and early 'thirties. Among them were Adalberto García de Mendoza, Eduardo García Máynez and Francisco Larroyo, the last of whom on his return from Marburg organized the neo-Kantian movement in Mexico. Moreover, in 1928-29 Samuel Ramos heard Georges Gurvitch lecture at the Sorbonne on the current tendencies in German philosophy. His lectures covered Husserl, Scheler, Lask, Hartmann and Heidegger. They were afterwards translated into Spanish and published in 1931 under the title *Las tendencias actuales de la filosofía alemana,* becoming therewith for the Spanish-speaking world the main secondary source of the major philosophical trends in Germany since Husserl. In addition, Antonio Caso stimulated some interest in contemporary German thought through his courses on Scheler and Husserl at the National University. So did his book on Husserl, published in 1934. Furthermore, the Spanish Civil War brought a number of talented refugees to Mexico, including José Gaos, Eduardo Nicol, Juan Roura-Parella, Luis Recaséns Siches (Guatemala-born), José Medina Echevarría, the late Joaquín Xirau and Juan David García Bacca. José Gaos has exerted the greatest influence on the present generation of Mexican students. As all of them had some affinity with Ortega's Madrid School and with its German background, their teaching has had the effect of intensifying the study of contemporary German thought as well as spreading the Orteguian point of view throughout Mexico.

145

To summarize the net effect of these various sources of intellectual importation upon the Mexican mind, one may divide twentieth-century philosophy in Mexico roughly into two periods. The first (1900-1925) can be said to have been inspired primarily by contemporary *French* ideas and the second (from 1925 on), by contemporary *German* ones via Spain. Such a shift in intellectual geography on the part of the present generation, to which the name of "Germanizantes" could be appropriately attached, is a more radical change of masters than the one experienced by the older generation of the Centenario (or Ateneo). For a change from Comte to Bergson, after all, is not so great as one from Bergson to Heidegger, especially if the continuity of Latin culture is assumed. On that assumption it would be difficult to believe that the "Germanizing" directions of recent thought in Mexico are actually more than skin-deep. Yet, skin-deep or not, they are there. Typical are the Scheler- and Hartmann-inspired ethics textbook in current use, *El secreto del bien y del mal* (1938), by José Romano Muñoz and the learned works in ethics and jurisprudence from the pen of Eduardo García Máynez, who studied abroad and came under the influence of Nicolai Hartmann at the University of Berlin and of Alfred von Verdross at the University of Vienna.

Reference has already been made to the rôle of Romano Muñoz and Ramos in introducing Ortega's thought to their generation of Contemporáneos. These two Mexicans belong, strictly speaking, to neither the past generation of the Centenario nor the present generation of the "Germanizantes," but constitute the local bridge from the former to the latter, with Ortega of Spain serving as foreign intermediary between Germany and Mexico. (How much twentieth-century German thought itself owes to Viennese intellectual circles is another story, of course.)

Ortega's influence in Mexico is seen not only in the general prestige that "Germanic culture" has steadily gained there since 1925, but also in the growing number of disciples who have learned to apply his specific "perspectivist" standpoint in philosophy to the Mexican scene. In view of the fact, then, that the contributions of his Mexican disciples reflect this double influence, they can be called "neo-Orteguians." But it is necessary to add at once that almost all they have done so far is to combine eclectically their master's thought with random ideas of the German phenomenological movement taken in the loose sense. In other words, they have not as yet assimilated one set of ideas to the other.

Moreover, even though it happens that the neo-Orteguians are exerting more influence on academic philosophy in Mexico than any other group at the moment, it would be a mistake to suppose that they are being left unchallenged there. Mexicans are born fighters and they take their ideas, like everything else, quite seriously. Not counting Vicente Lombardo Toledano and his Marxist comrades, who made hay while the sun of President Lázaro Cárdenas shone in the Zócalo (1934-40), the neo-Orteguians have been faced with a continual barrage of arguments from the neo-Kantians on the one side and the neo-Scholastics, the eternal defenders of *philosophia perennis,* on the other. In fact, the most belligerent group in Mexico until recently has been the neo-Kantian, whose organ is called *La Gaceta Filosófica.* If one wants to witness a "Freiburg versus Marburg" match in reverse, all he need do is consult the controversial writings of Francisco Larroyo and Guillermo Héctor Rodríguez, the leaders of the neo-Kantian movement in Mexico. (See the Bibliography for titles.) The pair swear by Hermann Cohen, the High Priest of neo-Kantianism. Their "criticist" attacks fall on both what they call the *perspectivismo romántico* of the neo-Orteguians and the *metafisicismo* of the Schoolmen.

As to the family squabbles among the Mexican neo-Kantians themselves, these are nothing compared to the controversies the different wings of the movement had originally in Germany. For one thing, all the neo-Kantians in Mexico seem to belong to the Right Wing (Marburg School). There is, however, one exception. The senior member of the group, Miguel Angel Cevallos, has written a slim *Ensayo sobre el conocimiento* (1944) from the standpoint of the Left Wing of the movement (the "critical realism" of the Würzburg School). But, alas, as it takes more than one swallow to make a spring, so it takes more than one feather to make a wing. Consequently, whatever may have been the fate of the German neo-Kantian movement elsewhere, it is its Right Wing (the "critical idealism" of the Marburg School) that has predominated in Mexico.

Turning to the Mexican neo-Scholastics, one finds that they are no more merciful to the neo-Kantian "critical idealists" than they are to the neo-Orteguian "perspective realists." Their lay leader is Oswaldo Robles at the National University, a devotee of Maritain's Paris School. Robles, who is fond of referring to himself as a "New Thomist" rather than a neo-Thomist, thinks that the worst devil in philosophy that ever lived was the philosopher from Koenigsberg. And despite the fact that Robles has been trying his utmost to make St. Thomas phenomenologically respectable, he insists, of course, that his compromise attempt at an *existencialismo augustino-tomista* stands poles apart from Heidegger's "nihilism in anguish."[3] By the way, this militant Thomist from Mexico City states in his introductory textbook, *The Main Problems of Philosophy* (English trans., 1946), that Nicolai Hartmann's theory of knowledge constitutes, in his opinion, "the soundest development of the phenomenological movement" (p. 57).

There is also some opposition in Mexico to Kant's influence from the Augustinian quarter. The best illustration from this anti-Kantian quarter comes from the pen of a lay disciple of the Bishop of Hippo, José Fuentes Mares. Fuentes is a young Mexican scholar whose principal work so far on Kant and modern liberalism is entitled *Kant y la evolución de la conciencia socio-política moderna* (1946). The book gets its inspiration from both Max Weber and Max Scheler. It is decidedly anti-liberal as well as anti-Kantian in tone. Its aim is "to relate the Reformation directly with liberalism." [4] Kant is interpreted as the ideologist of classical liberalism, the theoretical foundation of which is accused of pure formalism. As to the neo-Scholastic reaction to Ortega and his followers in Mexico, the most outspoken and forceful blows have come from a Mexican Jesuit by the name of José Sánchez Villaseñor. Incidentally, his critical study of Ortega's thought and its sources has been recently translated into English by Father Joseph Small and published under the title of *Ortega y Gasset, Existentialist* (1949).

Finally, the iconoclast in all these winds of doctrine in Mexico is a former neo-Kantian, Adolfo Menéndez Samará. This gentleman has of late gone the way of French existentialism. Yet it should be added that he is no atheistic kind of existentialist *à la* Sartre. His new master is the leader of the Catholic existentialists in France, Gabriel Marcel. Martin Heidegger is cavalierly dismissed as the "baroque" exponent of contemporary German philosophy in his recent book, *Menester y precisión del ser* (1946). The book merely sketches a theory of "the alter ego" similar to Scheler's and Sartre's. There is no reference, however, to the latter's ideas on the subject which appear in *L'Être et le Néant* (1943).

Ortega's general influence in Mexico—positive and negative—requires two final observations. The first can be derived from the latter-day resurrection of neo-Kantianism on Mexican soil, to wit, that there is no official coroner for the body philosophic. The second is as disconcerting to peace-loving people as the first is flattering to those who cherish their pet views at any cost. For the current philosophical situation in Mexico may be viewed as a three-way fight among neo-Orteguians, neo-Kantians, and neo-Scholastics—each group against the other two.

II. ORTEGA'S THOUGHT AND ITS REFLECTION IN MEXICO

Of the twofold influence of Ortega in present-day Mexico, attention has been directed upon his large-scale editorial efforts to bring contemporary German thought before the eyes of the Spanish-speaking world. The present concern must be with Ortega the philosopher proper and the impact of his ideas on Mexican minds. To facilitate the understanding of that impact, it would be advisable to examine first the origins and implications of his thought, especially since his general philosophical standpoint is not so well known to the English-speaking world as Bergson's, the major influence on the earlier generation of Caso and Vasconcelos. With his insight that human life is "biographical" in character, it seems appropriate to try to derive the main strains of his thought from the sources of intellectual autobiography scattered throughout his nimble and fluctuating writings.

Born in Madrid in 1883, Ortega completed his undergraduate work at a Jesuit school in Miraflores del Palo near Málaga. After being awarded the doctorate in philosophy and letters by the Central University of Madrid in 1904, he went to Germany for further study. He started at Leipzig, then attended the University of Berlin, and finished at Marburg, where he studied under "the great Hermann Cohen" and Paul Natorp, the leaders of the Right Wing of the neo-Kantian school. Ironically enough, Ortega reacted so much against his early training, which was steeped in both types of scholasticism—clerical (Jesuit) and secular (neo-Kantian) — that he has since become perhaps the most anti-scholastic mind in the contemporary world. In any case, it was at the University of Berlin, where he studied in 1906, that he came in contact with a current of thought which left a lasting imprint on his mind, notwithstanding his unwarranted afterthought to the effect that at the time "none of the philosophical chairs of the university was occupied by an outstanding scholar." [5]

Viewed historically, Ortega's general theory of philosophy, whose original name was *perspectivismo* (later changed to *raciovitalismo*), belongs to that humanistic, relativistic and activistic tendency which, coming under the influence of Renan, Bergson, Fichte and Nietzsche, "the super-seer" of *Lebensphilosophie,* became the predominant form of German thought at the turn of the century. Perspectivism can be traced back to Ortega's remotest ancestor, Protagoras, and nearest forerunner, Georg Simmel, an outstanding scholar (without a chair) at the University of Berlin during his post-graduate days. Ortega started where Simmel finished, that is, with "a metaphysics of life." [6] In his major philosophical work to date, *El tema de nuestro tiempo* (1923; English trans., *The Modern Theme,* 1931), Simmel is duly credited for seeing "more acutely than anyone else" [7] that human life has a *double character,* denominated *Mehr-Leben und Mehr-als-Leben* [8] in the *Lebensanschauung* (1918).

Ortega's corresponding formula for Simmel's double-aspect theory of human life—the immanent and the transcendent—appeared originally as a mere suggestion in the preface to his first book in 1914. It went as follows: *Yo soy yo y mi circunstancia.*[9] This proposition—"I am myself and my circumstance"—has since become the pivotal idea of his whole philosophy. What is its meaning? It can be approached from three angles: historical, analytical and ontological.

Historically speaking, the Orteguian *Meditations* begin with an *ego circumstans* instead of the *res cogitans* of Cartesian rationalism or the *ego cogitans* of post-Kantian idealism. Considered analytically, the basic proposition of the *Meditaciones del Quijote* means that my ego (the second *yo*) is no more than one ingredient in that radical reality "my life" (the first *yo*), whose other ingredient is the world around me (*mi circunstancia*). Finally, from the ontological standpoint, it signifies that man neither makes himself in a vacuum *ab intra* nor does circumstance make him a victim *ab extra*. For, inasmuch as each person must not only make himself continually, but must determine also *what* he is going to be in the light of circumstance, man is free "by compulsion," whether he likes it or not. In contrast to other beings, man is that "infinitely plastic entity" who is destined to be free, that is, capable of becoming other than what he was or is. Ortega, of course, is wise enough to realize that man's possibilities are limited to his particular circumstances. Nevertheless, the ultimate moral of his outlook is that no *a priori* "frontiers can be set to human plasticity." [10]

Even though Ortega's conception of life coincides in form with Simmel's, his point of view emerges, as will be seen, more historicist in content than that of the lonely Jew from Berlin. But, before the question of the influence of Simmel on Ortega is settled, it is indeed strange that the latter does not acknowledge his indebtedness to the former's important work in the field of epistemology. For perspectivism, which is, *sensu stricto,* a theory of knowledge in "culturist" dress—Ortega's jibes at the *ontophobia* of philosophy since Kant notwithstanding—what is it but a new name for Simmel's relativism? To be sure, the writer of *The Modern Theme,* defining relativism arbitrarily as the method opposed to rationalism, condemns it as irrational, but this criticism is irrelevant to Simmel's "functional" type of relativism. For the latter is just as conciliatory in temper as Ortega's attempt at a "synthesis" of the two opposed methods—rationalism and relativism—"of dealing with the antinomy between life and culture."[11] Not to speak of the stark confusion between a methodological and an epistemological issue underlying his alleged polarity of relativism and rationalism (relativism being not a way of acquiring truth but rather a theory of interpreting it), it seems odd that he should have been willing to set up a straw-doctrine of relativism when he had Simmel's relativistic position near at hand. Is it because Ortega suffers from "epistemophobia"? Or is it his linguistic device to conceal the relativistic foundation of his own perspectivism? At any rate, he distinguishes between "relativity" and "relativism," claiming in the appendix to *The Modern Theme* that an "impressive confirmation" of his theory is to be found in Einstein's physics.

This leads to a still stranger episode in the career of the Spanish thinker, namely, his intellectual kinship with a more prominent philosopher than Simmel at the University of Berlin, Wilhelm Dilthey, whom one of Ortega's translators mistakenly calls his "closest spiritual forebear." [12] The fault, in all fairness, however, is not entirely H. L. Nostrand's. For, in the essay on "History as a System" (1935), from which Mr. Nostrand derives his conclusion as to the influence of that German philosopher on the Spaniard, Ortega admits that Dilthey is "the writer to whom we owe more than to anyone else concerning the idea of life, and who is, to my mind, the most important thinker of the second half of the nineteenth century." [13] Nevertheless—and this is the difficulty—the slightly earlier Centennial essay on the German historicist himself, "Wilhelm Dilthey and the Idea of Life" (1933-34), states that Ortega did not become acquainted with his work until 1929, which is six years after the publication of *The Modern Theme*. If one takes the author's word that *The Modern Theme* was written without foreknowledge of Dilthey, the latter cannot be his closest spiritual forebear except in retrospect. Simmel, therefore, is really the man who fits the case in question.

Moreover, Ortega insists that the connection between Dilthey and himself is one of "a strange and disconcerting parallelism" of ideas. Their thought runs parallel; but for this very reason, he adds, their positions do not coincide. The Spaniard sees himself as a true successor of Dilthey, maintaining that his conception of *la razón vital* is "more advanced and plenary" than that of *historische Vernunft*. To put it in his own words: "With respect to the problem of life, *living reason* marks a higher level than *historical reason* at which Dilthey came to a halt."[14] Just as historicism is said to go beyond Kant's "pure reason," so Ortega believes that his "rational vitalism" goes beyond Dilthey's "historical reason," as far as the evolution of the idea of life is concerned. So much, then, for the line of descent between the philosopher from Madrid and his immediate predecessors from Berlin.

Despite the fact that Ortega has explicitly acknowledged his enormous debt to German philosophy in general and to Dilthey in particular, the spirit of his thought remains ineradicably Spanish, that is, deeply individualistic and impressionistic in tone. For one thing, the style of his thinking is definitely that of an essayist, not that of a "systemist." His proposed "Critique of Vital Reason," barely announced in *The Modern Theme* and nowhere developed to any considerable extent in any other writing of his, is only a *Kritik* in name. Though his philosophical ambition has been to complete Dilthey's work, his unfinished *Crítica de la razón vital* is still much more fragmentary than the latter's *Kritik der historischen Vernunft*. Besides, even if we grant his own confession that he "owes to Germany four fifths of his intellectual possessions," [15] there is still the other fifth to be taken into account. Ortega, in a word, is a typical Spaniard in mode of thought, *malgré lui*.

Friends and foes of the author agree (for different reasons, of course) that his philosophical thought bears close relations to *Existenzphilosophie*. This raises the question of the meaning of existentialism.[16] Existentialism has assumed different forms, especially in contemporary philosophy, but we may say that all of them share a fundamental preconception concerning the nature of *human* existence, namely, the *tragic* sense of life. Thus, for the present purposes, we can define existentialism in general as the theoretical expression of the tragic sense of life. A look at what Ortega had to say around 1932 about Martin Heidegger, his younger contemporary, may supply the missing link in the case for the existentialist vogue in present-day Mexico.

In a very telling footnote[17] to a Centennial article, "Goethe desde dentro" (1932), Ortega not only declares that he owes "very little" to the author of *Sein und Zeit* (1927), but goes so far as to affirm that there are "hardly one or two important concepts" in that "admirable book" which he had not anticipated by as much as thirteen years in the *Meditaciones del Quijote,* published at the outbreak of World War I. Above all, the Spaniard insists that his earlier notion of human life as *preocupación* approximates Heidegger's *Sorge*. So far, so good. But the author unwittingly spoils his own case by referring in the same footnote to another article of his called "The Sportive Origin of the State" (1924), in which he defends a diametrically opposite view, namely, that "life is an affair of flutes."[18] If life is that kind of affair, what is there for man to be concerned about? The "play" theory of life in "The Sportive Origin of the State" and in *The Modern Theme* is certainly inconsistent with the "preoccupation" idea in *Meditaciones del Quijote* and in "Goethe desde dentro."

Moreover, what is still more disconcerting is that the incompatibility between these two ideas of human existence is left unresolved within the very body of "The Sportive Origin of the State." Two passages from the article will prove the point.[19] The first, transcribed in the aforementioned footnote, sounds like Heidegger's notion of *ein Besorgen*: "For living means dealing with the world, turning to it, acting in it, being occupied with it." But the second passage, the thesis in fact of the article, is completely foreign to Heidegger's whole orientation: "Sportive activity seems to us the foremost and creative, the most exalted, serious, and important part of life, while labor ranks second as its derivative and precipitate. Nay more, life, properly speaking, resides in the first alone; the rest is relatively mechanic and a mere functioning." Ortega is apparently trying to have his "festive" cake and eat it. Consequently, is it any surprise that his anti-Cartesian Meditations on the nature of human life end in a stalemate? For given two Ortegas in one, no other outcome is possible.

Of the two polar ideas of life in Ortega's thought, the care and the care-free, it is only the first that has been assimilated by the Mexican mind. Mexicans experience too much of the tragic in their lives to swallow the sugar-coated pill of the Orteguian "sportive and festive sense of life."[20] Especially in a country like Mexico, where bullfighting takes on the proportions of a national cult—the cult of courage—man is not conceived after the Orteguian pose, as an eternal "athlete," but, to supply the appropriate simile, as an eternal *toreador*. To recall a point made in the introductory chapter, playing with a bull is not the same thing as playing with a ball! The bullfight, after all, symbolizes the final risk facing life—death itself—which is a serious affair of ultimate concern to every man. Life is not just an "affair of flutes" to mature people. Mexicans, not to mention the Spaniards themselves, could not and would not sympathize with Ortega's playing the flute, a variant of the classic fiddling, while Madrid burns.

Such negative reaction to the happy-go-lucky side of the Spaniard's philosophy of life explains in large part why his Mexican disciples are neo-Orteguians, rather than Orteguians proper. Not that they have actually articulated as yet their appraisal of their master in so many words, but the fact that Heidegger has been the most popular thinker in Mexico during the last decade or so indicates where they stand. They know instinctively that to conceive human life on the analogy of "sports" is shallow and narrow. They would feel that to invert the inveterate hierarchy of work and play is to pervert the ultimate meaning of human existence. Besides, Ortega in the rôle of a Carlyle in reverse, that is, as deifier of play, adds insult to injury by asserting that life, properly speaking, resides in sportive activity *alone*.

All this tacit antipathy on the part of the Mexicans to Ortega the intellectual playboy is, of course, intelligible. What is not intelligible, however, is why a man who pretends to be so aware of "Spain's misfortunes" should have been so unaware of the tragic significance, say, of the bullfight in his own country, the bullfighting center of the world. Had he taken Spain's national game, rather than her fiestas, more seriously, he would have been able to take life more seriously too. There is no greater irony in the whole of his philosophy than this, that as a Spaniard he does not metaphorically declare that *life is an affair of bullfights*. One may also wonder how a man who is "aware of the necessity of starting the analysis of the secret of life from the obvious, though unheeded, fact of the inevitability of death," [21] can have the nerve to utter without further ado and in almost the same breath that "life is an affair of flutes."

Considered from a psychological standpoint, it is fairly evident that Ortega's *sentido deportivo y festival de la vida* is a definite reaction against that masterpiece of his older contemporary and compatriot the late Miguel de Unamuno, *Del sentimiento trágico de la vida,* which appeared in 1913. Besides, one suspects that the man who preaches "the sportive and festive sense of life" does so with his tongue in his cheek. Yet, whatever the motivation, thinking is supposed to be a consistent business. Even the Emersonian jibe at consistency as "the hobgoblin of little minds" is directed against the "foolish" kind of consistency. When an artist like Cervantes dramatizes the pendulum of the human soul through his figures of Sancho Panza and Don Quixote, the result is an example of great literature; but when a man who tries to be a Cervantes in philosophy leaves those immortal symbols of the two opposite conceptions of life dangling in the air of discourse, that is an instance of great inconsistency. To write a *Don Quixote* is one thing; to write a *Meditations on Don Quixote,* quite another.

In the light of these paradoxical considerations, there remains a matter still more difficult to understand from the other side of the story, namely, why Unamuno, the Basque renowned for his appeal to "the tragic sense of life" and to the "flesh-and-bone man," should have been so neglected by Mexican scholars. Though Unamuno, an admirer of Kierkegaard, would doubtless attract the Mexican soul more than Ortega, the truth is that he has not exerted a noticeable influence on academic philosophy in Mexico. Finally, since what does and does not fit into the Mexican scheme of things is important, it may be noted in passing that Ortega's most widely-known book, *La rebelión de las masas* (1929; English trans., *The Revolt of the Masses,* 1932), is conspicuous by its almost complete absence in Mexican discussions. The reason should be obvious. Its attack on the democratic tradition of the common man (in Orteguian language, the "hyperdemocracy" of the "mass-man") is definitely out of harmony with the ideology of the

Mexican Revolution of 1910. Yet the irony of it all is that his followers in Mexico have exploited him to justify a nationalist movement which he himself would decry as a mass revolt.

Regardless of what is living and what is dead of the philosophy of Ortega from a Mexican point of view, his extensive influence in Mexico must still be accounted for. Briefly, José Ortega y Gasset is to the Mexican mind what William James is to the North American: a philosophical injection, so to speak, against the orthodox type of mentality. Perspectivism appeals, like pragmatism, to the same things: futurity, activity, relativity. And, strangely enough, the Spanish author is more consistent *as a pragmatist*—but only as such—than even the late John Dewey, in so far as his deliberate concern is only with the vital problems of men *in particular,* not with those of men *in general.* As there is no such entity for Ortega as "mankind at large" to which each one of us can address himself, it follows that the more nominalistic a pragmatist is, the more consistent he is. In other words, from the Orteguian point of view, the so-called "radical empiricism" of our leading pragmatists would not be radical enough. Moreover, Ortega would agree with the instrumentalist that man is in essence a "technician," but, at the same time, he would insist that human technology involves "the production of superfluities" [22] we need for well-being, not just the production of necessities for purposes of mere being or survival. Like Emerson's, Ortega's "man the technician" is the *self-made* man: *homo autofaber.* Here broods a long-waited declaration of cultural independence for a foreign-made land like Mexico to hearken to and herald.

Ortega is, incidentally, just as sensitive as Dewey to the customary charge of being anti-intellectualist. For he sees the appeal to "vital reason" as actually an attempt on his part at reconciling the major antinomy of "pure reason" at one extreme and "vital impulse" at the other. Aiming as it does at saving both the rationality and spontaneity of human life, his method can hardly be called a revolt against reason without qualification. The whole point of his doctrine of *la razón vital* is precisely to bring together the two concepts usually put asunder by modern thought, namely, life and reason.[23] For he would argue, to paraphrase Kant, not only that reason without life is empty, but also, conversely, that life without reason is blind. In short, Ortega is not really an *anti*-intellectualist; to be exact, he is a *non*-intellectualist. As he explains:[24]

> The irrationality of the principles of knowledge, with which rationalism is faced in the end, is due to the fact that reason is understood as "pure reason," detached and isolated. But when "pure reason" is founded on the totality of "living reason," the irrationalism to which proud reason sees itself condemned dissolves and turns into clear and ironical rationalism. For many years I have therefore described my own philosophical standpoint as a *ratio-vitalism*. My book *El tema de nuestro tiempo* (*The Modern Theme*), Madrid, 1923, presents the issue of embedding pure reason in living reason as the theme of our time.

The subsequent development of neo-Orteguianism in Mexico makes one thing clear, namely, that what his Mexican disciples have learned most of all from their Spanish master is "the epistemological justification of a national philosophy," to repeat the key phrase from the pen of Samuel Ramos, the initial spokesman for the Generation of Contemporáneos. This lesson involved essentially a radical change in the conception of philosophy itself. This requires some elaboration.

It has been said that, according to Ramos, his generation was shown how to harmonize philosophy with its nationalistic aspirations by incorporating Ortega's conception of "the historicity of philosophy" defended in *The Modern Theme*. The end of that small volume of essays calls for "a radical reform in philosophy."[25]

Every philosophical position carries with it tacitly or expressly a certain conception of what philosophy is or should be. In order to arrive at the Orteguian conception, his doctrine of perspectivism must first be defined.

Perspectivism, in brief, is the theory which holds that since reality is composed, like a landscape, of an "infinite number of perspectives," some of which we come to know through the "selective" medium of "vital reason," therefore, reality does not possess in itself, "independently of the point of view from which it is observed, a physiognomy of its own." [26] In accordance with this infinite-aspect theory of reality, the animus of which is to banish the category of "substance" from the cosmic map, there is no "standard landscape" *à la* Platonist over and above the determinate appearances we actually experience. Perspectives do not distort reality; they constitute it. Truths are points of view, all of which are "equally veridical and authentic." A point of view is not true or false in the absolute sense. Having a point of view is like having a wife: it is for better or for worse. Accordingly, to err is to pretend to possess more than a point of view. Error is pride in theory, the cardinal sin of man the knower. There is no divine forgiveness for such sin. Ortega's God is "not a rationalist" either, but also a point of view. In other words, truth and error, like life and death, are matters of history and history is a matter of perspectives. Gone forever is Truth with a capital T!

Perspectivism, on examination, turns out to be a new name for the epistemological theory of "Objective Relativism" (Lovejoy) or "Perspective Realism" (McGilvary). Wherein then, one may ask, lies its originality? It is in that Ortega takes one more step than Protagoras: *each* man is the measure of all things. But the Orteguian *homo* is no man without a country. To counteract the solipsistic implication of his "radical reality," *mi vida,* and counterattack Leibniz's *Monadology* (the little classic which, written exactly two hundred years before the publication of *Meditaciones del Quijote,* is a defense of perspectivism in rationalist terms), the Spanish writer restores to individuals their *national* "windows," that is, their *national* "perspectives." Consequently, in the end the Protagorean *homo mensura* gets historicized and nationalized into *homo hispanus mensura,* etc. Ortega is without any doubt *the* philosopher of the *modern* theme *par excellence!*[27]

The question of the implications of this way of thinking for the nature of philosophy now asserts itself. What does Orteguian perspectivism do to philosophy? It changes her in *form,* from something abstract and eternal—*la belle dame sans point de vue*— to something concrete and historical. Ortega dares to accuse the traditional conception of philosophy of "utopianism" and "uchronianism," the original sin of the pure rationalist. Its classic model is Spinoza, the philosopher of a Reality which is "nowhere" and "nowhen" in particular but "everywhere" and "everywhen" in general. In contrast, the perspectivist literally puts philosophy in her place and time: "After twenty-five centuries of mental training to grasp reality *sub specie aeternitatis,* we must make a new start and develop an intellectual technique for detecting it *sub specie instantis.*"[28] Here is indeed a more radical Luther than Dewey ever dreamed of being in his *Reconstruction in Philosophy* (1920). For Ortega, to put it in Dilthey's language, is an inverted Spinoza or Malebranche in "philosophy of philosophy."

In addition, perspectivism brings about a complete reform in the *content* of philosophy. Henceforth the prime concern of the philosopher is no longer with the ways of Nature, but with those of Culture. It is precisely the cultural life of man which Ortega the *Kulturphilosoph* urges us to make the proper study of philosophy. So much so that he bestows ontological "primacy" upon that life. Now, since the Orteguian Meditations are addressed exclusively to the ways of human culture, it follows that philosophy of nature has to yield its place of honor to philosophy of culture. In *The Modern Theme* the latter is called, after Scheler, "Meta-history," a discipline which bears the same relation to concrete histories "as physiology to the clinic." It should have been de-nominated, to be more exact, "Metaculture." Yet, whatever be its name, the fact remains that Metaphysics (in the traditional sense) is pronounced dead by Ortega. Thus our twentieth-century coroner from Madrid does to Metaphysics what the nineteenth-century Nietzsche did to God. All of which means that, given the "metacultural" nature of philosophy itself, his Mexican dis-ciples now have the sanction to go their ways and, what is more important, to travel on their own.

III. THE WORK OF MEXICAN NEO-ORTEGUIANS

With this critical account of Ortega's thought and its general repercussions in contemporary Mexico completed, it is now time to examine those specific studies in the philosophy of culture which have been published by those Mexican scholars who have come under his direct or indirect inspiration. In this connection, attention will fall on the relevant material of the following four Mexican neo-Orteguians: Samuel Ramos, Leopoldo Zea, Ed-mundo O'Gorman and Justino Fernández.

Historically speaking, the pioneer in "the philosophy of Mex-ican culture" [29] is Samuel Ramos. Three stages may be discerned in the development of his thought: (1) the positivist, (2) the prag-matist and (3) the perspectivist. From his first book, a collection of essays published in 1928 under the title of *Hipótesis,* it is pos-sible to trace these three stages. During his student days in the picturesque Mexican town of Morelia he came under the influence of the local positivist, José Torres. The volume just cited closes with an essay, "Mi experiencia pragmatista," in which the author confesses his affinity for pragmatism and for Antonio Caso, its "champion" then in Mexico. There he admits also that he originally saw in pragmatism the way out of his own spiritual crisis, which he felt as early as 1916, between Thomistic scholasticism on the one hand and Comtian positivism on the other. But, as the beginning of the chapter has already brought out, Caso proved to be such a disappointment to Ramos that Ortega finally won out in the end. So much so that he considers himself the only member of his generation capable of looking at Caso objectively or from a "distant perspective." [30]

Even though Ramos reports in an autobiographical mood at the close of his *History of Philosophy in Mexico* (1943) that his Generation of Contemporáneos was dissatisfied with the "philosophical romanticism" of Caso and Vasconcelos, still we must not forget that elsewhere he shows sympathy for the latter's "philosophy of the Ibero-American race" and his "genuinely Mexican" [31] work in the field of educational administration, all of which must have prepared the ground for his own interest in the philosophy of Mexican culture. Ramos tends to emphasize Ortega at the expense of Vasconcelos, but this is analogous to the Biblical case of the prophet who has no honor in his own country. Be that as it may, Ramos tells us that he found a "norm" applicable to Mexico in Ortega's pivotal idea: *Yo soy yo y mi circunstancia*. Thus Ramos learns from Orteguian perspectivism that, just as "there is a Chinese perspective which is fully as justified as the Western," [32] so by the same token there must be a *Mexican* point of view which is fully as justified as the European. Hence Mexican philosophy, like charity, must begin at home in order to find its individuality.

In 1934 Ramos published a much-discussed book entitled *El perfil del hombre y la cultura en México,* the express object of which is to explore "Mexican circumstances" in a philosophical manner so as to provide a solid foundation for the future reconstruction of the Mexican way of life. Its purpose is more to rectify than to justify the ways of Mexico to man. In fact, the method it attempts to apply to the Mexican situation is, interestingly enough, Alfred Adler's psychoanalysis.

In accordance with this *psicoanálisis del mexicano,* the love of imitation is at the root of all evil in Mexico as a nation. *Homo Mexicanus* has been living, alas, in a simian world, trying to copy European culture at any cost. The stock example of such *mimetismo* is to be found in the field of constitutional law throughout the nineteenth century, a time when the Mexican government blindly borrowed French legal documents and the U. S. Constitution, paying no attention to the peculiarity of Mexico's circumstances and her *mestizo* pattern of culture. The author insists that as a result of the imitative process the Mexicans have acquired an inferiority complex, their natural reaction being one of looking down with suspicion on the copies they had and, conversely, looking up with envy at the originals they did not have.

Given the Adlerian approach to the problem, the solution Ramos offers, briefly stated, is this: Mexicans must henceforth *be* Mexicans, that is, neither Mexicanists *à la* Aztec nor Europeanists. Just as Ortega, to generalize, had resolved the antinomy between life and reason (culture) in *The Modern Theme* by means of his synthesis of "living reason," so the author of *The Profile of Man and Culture in Mexico* applies the same principle of polarity to Mexico and urges his countrymen to adopt a "living culture."[33] Incidentally, the Mexican writer uses the more fitting phrase *cultura viviente* for Ortega's *razón vital* or *razón viviente.*

Ramos finishes his character sketch of the Mexican soul with a plea that a new humanistic orientation is needed in the schools of Mexico to counteract the Yankee menace of the "instrumental conception of man"[34] underlying the materialistic civilization of the "Colossus of the North." (The plea obviously records a violent reaction against Dewey's influence on Mexican education at the time.) The appeal to a "new humanism" is touched upon subsequently in *Más allá de la moral de Kant* (1938) and developed as a program of "philosophical anthropology" (Scheler) in *Hacia un nuevo humanismo* (1940). Both volumes attack "the naturalistic conception of man" [35] with weapons borrowed from Ortega, contemporary German philosophy and Viennese psychoanalysis.

The Ramos of the present generation in Mexico is Leopoldo Zea. Praising his elder colleague for championing the cause of *la mexicanidad,* he has been chiefly interested in showing that the Mexican mind is representative of an Hispano-American *logos.* [36] The analogy with Ortega is striking. Just as the latter sees the Spaniard from the broader perspective of "European man," similarly Zea regards the Mexican as a species of "American man." And what corresponds in theme to Ortega's "Unity and Diversity of Europe" is "The Two Americas," originally published in the Mexican journal *Cuadernos Americanos* in 1944. [37]

Having made a thorough study of the career of positivism in Mexico, the goal of whose educational policy was to "anglicize" the Mexicans, Zea is led to generalize that the trouble with the Latin-American soul originates in its attempts "to sacrifice its own ideal of life" for the North American ideal of "material comfort." [38] In trying to acquire capacities alien to her, Latin America has naturally failed, with the inevitable result that she has lost confidence in herself. Mexico, having the *Coloso del Norte* next door, is the clearest example in the Western Hemisphere of what happens to a country when it suffers from an inferiority complex on a national scale. And the pity of it all, he contends, is that the Mexican positivists during the heyday of the Porfirist Era were so ready to believe that Anglo-America possessed the only key to happiness that they played directly into their enemy's hands.

They failed completely to realize that as there is no royal road to truth, so there is none to happiness. This criticism of the ideology of Mexican positivism implies that no meeting of the two Americas is possible without the presupposition of a plurality of ideals. Zea's axiological pluralism is doubtless consistent with the epistemological pluralism of Orteguian perspectivism.

Given the historical fact of Hispano-America's original dependency on European culture and her subsequent fear of "Yankee imperialism," Zea concludes that her basic problem is to achieve cultural independence. He points to the current striving for cultural emancipation on the part of Latin Americans as evidence for the presence of a new phenomenon in America, namely, the consciousness of an *American* culture as such. To make this phenomenon intelligible, he goes to the history of ideas in Latin America and selects as the contributing factors the philosophy of the Enlightenment and historicism, the two liberalizing "stages" of Hispano-American thought. According to Zea, it was through the first that Latin America was able during the last century to discover her "political personality," and it is through the second, still in the making, that she will eventually come to recognize her "spiritual personality." For the historicist mode of thinking, with its stress on the relativity of truths, has come to justify the urge for the cultural emancipation of America, its central message being that each generation must make or remake its own table of values and its own table of truths.[39]

Zea's *En torno a una filosofía americana* (1945) prepares the way for making America's own table of truths and values by inquiring into "the possibility of an American philosophy."[40] It is important to note in passing that the author uses the adjective "American" to denote *both* Americas, North and South. Even though this is the case, most of his account, however, is actually concerned with the second, presumably because as a Mexican he knows his own half better and is naturally more interested in her. Note should also be taken in passing that his theme is more extensive, not to say more ambitious, than Ramos', but less so than Northrop's.

The monograph *Concerning an American Philosophy* is divided neatly into three parts, opening with the disconcerting question: is an *American* philosophy possible? Zea's answer is affirmative and his reason may be put in terms of our popular proverb: necessity is the mother of invention. In the author's own words:[41]

> The men or peoples who have had philosophy have had it because they needed it; those who have not, because they did not need it. The latter is the case with America. She does not have her own philosophy because she has not been in need of it, just as she has not needed her own culture; yet this should not be taken to mean that she will not attain them if she needs them. Her failure up to now in such an enterprise is not to be ascribed to her lack of capacity but to their being unnecessary.

That is, a negative instance of philosophy or culture is proof merely of the absence of environmental necessity or the appropriate "circumstances," not proof of hereditary incapacity to philosophize.

This ultra-pragmatic conception of philosophy and culture is clearly at odds with Aristotle's leisure view and would probably have made even our own John Dewey blush a little at its implication. At any rate, Zea the Hispano-American and Dewey the Anglo-American meet at least on the crucial point of starting as instrumentalists. To that extent both must have, on Zea's thesis, a common circumstance, if not a common faith—the common circumstance being that America is, historically considered, a European dependency. The consequence of such a common ground in theory and common circumstance in fact would be tremendous for political action, since they would make possible the meeting of

North and South on some solid foundations instead of the customary romanticizing sand on which the two Americas have tried to build their foreign relations in the past. Moreover, whether Zea is right or not as to the origin of ideas in human experience, his whole approach should lead us to question our usual preconceptions about the "impractical" character of the Latin-American mind.

It is safe to say that Zea's "circumstantialism" is derived illegitimately from Ortega's fundamental intuition of human life: *Yo soy yo y mi circunstancia.* The derivation is illegitimate precisely because that philosopher from Madrid actually defends in the important essay, "Man the Technician," [42] the opposite of the thesis that necessity is the mother of invention. From the Orteguian standpoint, the trouble with Zea's position concerning the origin of culture in general and of philosophy in particular would be that it unwittingly presupposes the utilitarian interpretation of life, which rests upon the Darwinian theory of evolution. According to the Madrid philosopher, the Darwinian view is a "current myth" which has already been exploded by recent investigations in the field of biology and history.[43]

Having granted that an *American* philosophy is possible, the Mexican author raises his next issue in Part One: what *kind* of philosophy is accessible to us as Americans? The answer is simply what one would expect from the general thesis of the booklet, to wit, not any kind, but a particular philosophy arising out of our special circumstances as Americans living in a New World. Zea is keenly aware that the particularist position he is defending goes against the universalist grain of traditional philosophy, which looks at things *sub specie aeternitatis.* The author passes judgment on such views and finds them pretentious and contradictory. In spite of all its extravagant claims to be the possessor of eternal and immutable truths, philosophy becomes nothing but a comedy of errors when it dawns upon us that those claims actually conflict.

Besides, the traditional conception of philosophy flies in the face of the nature of man. What is man, then? According to Zea, "Man is an historical entity, that is, an entity whose essence is change. The man of today is not the same as the one of yesterday, nor will he be tomorrow's." Hence, given the historicity of man, it follows that "the truth of each man or generation comes to be nothing but the expression of a determinate conception of the world and of life." [44] What shall it profit a philosophy which gainsays the whole world and loses its own soul? Philosophy must be shorn of its pretensions at doing the impossible and, instead, must move humbly among us with an eagerness for solving the concrete problems of men.

Far from reaching universal truths, philosophy can only attain partial or "circumstantial" truths, all of which stamp it with a peculiar character, such as Greek, French, German or English. For Zea there is really no such thing as philosophy pure and simple. What there is always has a predicate, Greek or otherwise. Since we Americans are not Greeks, our philosophy cannot be Greek. It must be *American,* in spite of ourselves and of our devotion to the glory that was Greece. For new circumstances teach not only new duties but also new verities. We *can* philosophize, of course, but Zea warns us not to do it mechanically. All we need do is *think through* our specific problems and the resulting philosophy will be *American,* willy-nilly. But, there is the difficulty, or, as Cantinflas says in Mexico: *Ahí está el detalle!*

Although philosophy is always "circumstantial," notwithstanding the claims of the philosophers to the contrary, it can never quite get itself to accept in theory what it is known to be in fact. This situation generates its fundamental paradox: "Philosophy is not satisfied with reaching a circumstantial truth, but tries to attain a universal truth." [45] How can its relativist results, for which alone there is empirical evidence, conform to the absolutist quest for certainty native to philosophizing itself?

Zea attempts to resolve the philosopher's predicament by admitting that while "there is a single absolute reality, what is neither absolute nor single are the points of view from which this reality may be grasped," and by recognizing that all men, whether Jews or Gentiles, Greeks or Romans, Europeans or Americans, "participate in a circumstance common to them: humanity." [46] Reality, to be sure, like St. Peter's God, is no respecter of persons and is democratic enough to endow no one of us with a privileged point of view. Such metaphysical egalitarianism and the limitations inherent in all men make it possible, after all, for different individuals and peoples to work together towards mutual understanding. Without the first or leveling component we would have a veritable Tower of Babel; without the second or limiting component, a continual Armageddon.

Zea is too much a humanist to draw the naturalistic implication of his thought. For, if one declares with him that the "human circumstance" is what binds all men together, one should by the same token declare that what binds all men and everything else together is what may be called the "natural circumstance." Otherwise our humanism will be half-headed, if not half-hearted, and not be as good a guide to mankind as naturalism. Man must be given his proper place within Nature, if he is not to stick out like a sore thumb.

As Part One of the monograph tries to show in what sense we *can* philosophize, Part Two deals with why we *should*.

Since it may be inferred from the "circumstantialist" point of view that any particular philosophy whatsoever is born out of the problems of human experience, what is the "vital situation" which characterizes the American scene? A sincere description of our circumstances points without question to the cultural dependency of the Americas on European culture. This basic fact of our history is the root of the American malady. Here is where Zea follows Ramos and turns psychoanalyst.

We Americans are, culturally speaking, children of Europe, yet unfortunately we do not feel that we are her legitimate offspring. Rather, we feel that European culture is too much for us. Out of this feeling of inferiority arises "the maladjustment of the American man." [47] The trouble lies in the fact that we put the cart before the horse: instead of adapting European culture to ourselves and our circumstances, we do it the other way around. We imitate Europeans but fail miserably because we are, whether we like it or not, people living in a New World under conditions differing from the Old. The moral of Zea's story is that the sooner we recognize our folly, the sooner will we be saved.

The diagnosis of the American malady, whose Hispano-American variety goes under the name of *criollismo,* is carried on from the biological language of "maladjustment" to the psychological language of "inferiority complex." This complex, according to Zea, originates from the great gap between Europe's original dream of establishing a Promised Land in the New World and the stark reality of that land. It is at this point that a highly controversial comparison is made of the Anglo-American and the Latin-American expressions of their alleged feeling of inferiority. The relevant passage is not only amusing but instructive as well. Note how a typical Mexican reacts to the "Colossus of the North": [48]

> The feeling of inferiority manifests itself in Anglo-America through the craving to reproduce on a bigger scale what is done by Europe. Anglo-America prides herself in being the future of Western Culture. All her propaganda—in newspapers, magazines, movies, etc.—is animated by this urge. She tries to make a second Europe out of America,

but with larger dimensions. The gigantic, the colossal, that is, the quantitative, is what preoccupies her most. She strives to obtain all this through money and a bigger and better technology. Yet at the bottom there brews a feeling of inferiority. . . . For all this cult of the enormous . . . is but a mask, a form of compensating for a certain timidity, a lack of courage to stand on one's own feet. It seems that North Americans don't want to give up their childhood. They rest content with surprising and amazing their elders with efforts that appear greater than their abilities. The Hispano-American, in contrast to the North American, does not hide his feeling of inferiority. On the contrary, he exhibits it and is continually defaming himself. He is always making evident his incapacity to create. He tries nothing on his own and is satisfied with assimilating another's culture. But for doing so he feels inferior, like a servant who wears the suit of his master.

Latin Americans, then, suffer from the inferiority complex of bastards; North Americans, from that of brats.

All of this looks rather dark for both sides of the Rio Grande. Of course, no one should be very astonished at what happens to the American soul when it undergoes psychoanalysis, Adlerian or otherwise, but what is most disconcerting about Zea's strictures against it is that one does not expect his conclusion from the original premise of the inevitability of philosophy defended in Part One of his study. It is to be remembered that he cavalierly contends that philosophy will out whenever and wherever necessary and that its absence signifies its non-necessity. If that were the case, however, why should he be obliged to prescribe a pound of cure for the American soul today when an ounce of prevention could have saved it long before? Why is it that America did not develop a philosophy of her own before she fell victim to the assumed inferiority complex? To answer that she did not turn to philosophy because she did not need to is begging the question. The historical fact is that she did lend an ear to whatever philosophy

suited her interests, individual and social. Is philosophy like a
suit of clothes that can be put on or taken off in accordance with
the "circumstances"? That sounds absurd. Moreover, experience
and history teach that philosophy, whether it is our own or not,
is no panacea for what ails us. More things are wrought by
philosophy than this world dreams of, but not so many as Zea
dreams of. He seems to be making not only a virtue of the necessary, in so far as he believes that philosophy will inevitably be
born to those who need it, but is also making a vice of the unnecessary, in so far as such a condition is accompanied by living
off the fat of borrowed culture. To be more concrete, the argument seems to be that since Europe supplied us originally with the
tools of culture, consequently, it was unnecessary for us to think
on our own. This state of affairs, nevertheless, made us eventually
parasites of European culture and we are paying for it at present
in the form of an inferiority complex. Zea's "circumstantialism"
turns out, on examination, to be a boomerang.

Having diagnosed the sickness of the American soul as one of
sentimiento de inferioridad, Doctor Zea proceeds to prescribe the
cure at the end of Part Two. The way out of our predicament is,
in brief, to acquire a sense of responsibility.[49] Our coming of age
depends on the honest recognition of our *American* circumstances.
But the awareness of our irreducible *American* character should
not be pushed so far as to deny our cultural relations with Europe.
Hence, Zea warns, we should be *Americans,* not *Americanists.*
Should this solution be considered too irrelevant in an Atomic
Age, it could be easily replied that there is nothing better than
confessing our own soul *per interim.* One could hardly deny the
cathartic value of spelling out our own equation.

Part Three outlines the task for a possible American philosophy in the near future. It reassures us that the fact of our not
having had our own philosophy in the past is no sign of our

incapacity, but merely implies its not having been necessary for us at the time. In contrast, the present situation unmistakably calls for a New World Philosophy. All is not right with the world. Europe is suffering from a serious crisis and we in America must not allow her to succumb.

Our job as American philosophers, Zea concludes in a conciliatory mood, is to continue working on the abstract or universal themes of Western culture along with those germane to our circumstance as residents of the New World. Both themes are closely connected and occasion "the one and only theme" of all genuine thinking, which is "that of Man."[50] The specific conceptions of man emerging therefrom will be marked with, first, a "national character," such as North American, Mexican, etc., due to regional conditions, and secondly, a "continental character" due to our common lot. Our particular philosophies, to repeat, will be American in spite of ourselves because they will be determined by our own "circumstances," whatever these may specifically be.

From the observation that our systems have in the past been "bad copies" of European philosophy, Zea infers, optimistically enough, that therein "is hidden perhaps our American character. To admit that we are a bad copy does not signify that we admit our being inferior, but simply that we are different." [51] Incidentally, what one may call for Zea the "copy" theory of culture does not seem to have the serious limitations of the "copy" theory of knowledge, because once we are willing to admit that we are bad copies of European culture, we shall no longer be infected with cynicism —which is to action what scepticism is to understanding—but shall instead bring into focus our own perspectives on life and thus create our own patterns of culture. At any rate, to make explicit our ideological differences from other men, such as the European or the Asiatic, is the specific task we should take upon ourselves immediately. If we are to be successful in carrying out this program, we must see to it that our intellectuals come out of their proverbial ivory towers and coordinate ideas with reality. Without the coordination of theory and practice, no meeting of North and South America is possible. *Periculum in mora.*

While Leopoldo Zea approaches the theme of America as a neo-Orteguian "circumstantialist," Edmundo O'Gorman treats the same theme as a neo-Orteguian historicist. His small but stimulating volume, *Fundamentos de la historia de América* (1942), is "a first attempt at a synthesis aimed at establishing the foundations of the *History of America*." [52] In O'Gorman's opinion, an adequate history of America still needs to be written, because almost all the available material on the subject suffers from a "notorious onesidedness." He complains that the incorporation of America into Western culture has been investigated to date almost exclusively from the political point of view with the same methods and assumptions used in the natural sciences. Though studies abound, to be sure, on the various phases of the discovery of America—military, political, economic, religious—we still lack a comprehensive perspective on the question of why Europe conquered America when she did and of how she carried through the process of her incorporation in terms of their common vital interests at the time. O'Gorman calls the answer that must be given to this decisive question the "Philosophical Conquest of America."

The Preface rejects the "naturalist type" of explanation on the ground that the so-called *natural* "motives" of human nature—ambition, power, greed, etc.—do not really explain why the European was interested in conquering America. For it could be easily counterargued that, say, indifference and indolence, are just as "natural" to man as ambition and greed. How can a naturalistic biology or psychology settle *which* motive predominates in a given situation? Therefore, if we want to make intelligible that complex series of events historians call the discovery of America, we must delve into the peculiar historical situation constituting European life during the fifteenth and sixteenth centuries and see how that situation is reflected in Europe's incorporation of America on the ideological level. Like F. S. C. Northrop, O'Gorman urges us to go back to the intellectual sources that entered into the cultural meeting of Europe and America.

As an illustration of what he means by the philosophical sources of Euro-America, the *De unico vocationis modo* by Fr. Bartolomé de Las Casas may be selected for critical examination. In Chapter II, on O'Gorman's authority, that unorthodox Spanish Thomist of the early sixteenth century in New Spain was mentioned as a precursor of Descartes. How does the Mexican historian connect the two men with respect to the present theme of the origins of Euro-American culture?

According to O'Gorman, around the time of Columbus the idea of America raised a great doubt in the European mind as to the validity of the current belief in the uniformity of Nature. Was the American world identical in essence with the European? Did the American belong to the same species of *homo sapiens* as the European? So prevalent was the doubt that it was soon communicated in the original phrase coined by the European to denote America, "the New World." It gave rise to a fervid polemic from which we have not as yet recovered. To allay such a state of uncertainty over the nature of *Homo Americanus,* O'Gorman continues, the European ventured across the seas to find out what it really was. Thus the philosophy of Descartes, symbol of modern rationalism, becomes the theoretical epitomization of the doubting European.

The most ingenious feature of the author's account is the close connection he tries to establish between "the anguish of the state of doubt" on the part of the European towards America and the Cartesian method of universal doubt. The implication seems to be that the European was able through the Cartesian *Cogito* to rationalize the existence of America as follows: I think of America, therefore she exists.[53] But, it is added, this purely rational proof was not sufficient to satisfy the empirical demands of Father Las Casas' sceptical contemporaries. To meet their challenge, he was obliged to put to the test his "evangelizing hypothesis" about the common essence of man by conducting an experiment at Vera Paz, Guatemala.

The Vera Paz experiment is, for three reasons, highly significant to O'Gorman. In the first place, it illustrates what he means by the *Conquista filosófica de América.* In the second place, its scientific approach to the study of human nature is testimony of the modernity of Father Las Casas' mind. Finally, and most importantly, it was through this experiment that America literally obtained her first "European *naturalization* papers." [54] Lest one be too optimistic, however, it must be added that inasmuch as the Renaissance polemic over the rationality of the American Indian had a "double aspect," the Vera Paz experiment settled only the question of his "humanity." The other aspect, "the inferiority of the American," was to lie dormant until it raised its ugly head in the eighteenth century. Letting sleeping dogs lie and returning to the *Foundations of American History,* one may conclude that in this work the author offers a rather novel perspective on how America came to be, a "vision of America" tinged with the anguished spirit of Heidegger.

While the book of O'Gorman's just passed in brief review is concerned with providing the proper foundations to the particular history of America, his *Crisis y porvenir de la ciencia histórica* (1947) is concerned with the more general question of how "an authentic science of history ought to be grounded."[55] Here the author generalizes from his earlier work and emerges with a neo-Orteguian conception of history. The problem of determining the nature of history is treated polemically at first, beginning with a distinction derivable from Ortega between "historiography" and "historiology." By the former, O'Gorman means the "traditional or naturalistic" conception of history, the model exponent of which is Leopold von Ranke, the German founder of scientific history in the last century; by the latter, he means the existentialist view of contemporary historicism, whose outstanding champion to him is Martin Heidegger.

The principal trouble with Ranke, according to O'Gorman, is that he "reifies history." For a "naturalist historiography" removes the historical from history, the *temporalidad* of "our life," by failing to make a radical distinction "between the human past and the *things* of Nature." Whereas natural things *have* a history, man *is* history. To the naturalist conception of man, "man a thing," there corresponds a naturalist conception of history, "history a thing." Ranke's notion that the task of the historian is to narrate "what actually happened" is not only pretentious; it is irrelevant to human weal and woe, because "the past is something which does not and can not have any influence upon life," to quote that German's own words. This Rankian passage constitutes the postulate of traditional historiography. The postulate itself involves a belief in "the past" as something existing independently of our present life, that is, it involves an epistemology which, like Locke's belief in the external world, leads inevitably to scepticism. Therefore, O'Gorman argues that the current "crisis" of history as a science is due precisely to its underlying naturalistic presupposition, the evident implication of which is "historical relativism."[56]

The whole point of his recent volume is to show that historical relativism and contemporary historicism are, despite the appearances to the contrary, "alien" to each other. His chief argument is that the usual charge of scepticism leveled at historicism belongs properly to the naturalistic conception of history, because the absolute presupposed by the latter—Nature—is ultimately unknowable. Although one may seriously question, of course, whether *all* forms of naturalistic philosophy necessarily imply agnosticism, there is no doubt that *some* do. To the extent that some do, O'Gorman is right; but to the extent that some do not, he is wrong.

Having disposed of his naturalistic enemy, O'Gorman proposes that the crisis of history as a science can be met in the future only if we recover consciousness of our own historical character and rediscover that Orteguian "absolute" which is our "own life." To find such an absolute, he goes to Heidegger's doctrine of history and elaborates on it critically. According to the "historiological" view of history, the essence of man and the essence of history coincide. The property of *historicidad* belongs to man alone. "Man is capable of apprehending history *because* he is historical." Historiological cognition is nothing but the present recognition of ourselves in the past seen with a "future perspective" in mind. Whereas *la historiografía* is the unauthentic science which teaches us to "forget ourselves," *la historiología* teaches us just the opposite.[57]

History and pure mathematics are the two poles of scientific knowledge proper, ranging from the maximum of concreteness in the first to the maximum of abstractness in the second. (Interestingly enough, the late Morris R. Cohen arrived at the same conclusion as a naturalist in *The Meaning of Human History,* published in 1947.)[58] Consequently, since reality is historical in essence, it follows that a genuine science of history possesses "an ontological primacy over all the other sciences."[59] The only other discipline which surpasses the study of history in primacy is, of course, philosophy itself, whose function is to inquire into "historicity as such." This raises the question of the relation between history and philosophy. Given the foregoing considerations, it should be obvious that their relation is reciprocal; and what should be even more obvious is that any attempt to divorce the two is illogical for O'Gorman.

Of all the Mexican neo-Orteguians, Edmundo O'Gorman is the most adroit in the utilization of source materials. To give one or two examples, in his study of Las Casas he borrows from the extensive research work done by Lewis Hanke, though he differs from the former director of the Hispanic Foundation in his interpretation of that great defender of the American Indian. For his knowledge of Heidegger's philosophy O'Gorman is heavily indebted to his teacher José Gaos, originally a disciple of Ortega's and now the leading Spanish existentialist in Mexico. One may select for a test case of O'Gorman's adroitness the way he handles Heidegger.

Although he sings the praises of *Sein und Zeit,* calling it "a guide for the authentic life," he declares himself independent of its author in several respects. In the first place, he criticizes that German existentialist for failing to guarantee to history its own autonomy as a science and imposing upon it a set of categories from the outside. That is to say, he is opposed to having historical science explained away and swallowed into ontology. Secondly, he finds fault with Heidegger's stubborn attempt at keeping value judgments out of ontological issues, contending that the authentic mode of being is actually superior to the unauthentic. Finally, he believes that Heidegger's definition of man as *Sein zum Tode* suffers from a "manifest onesidedness." Not that he denies the tremendous power of this insight; rather what he denies is that man is *nothing but* what the definition affirms. In fact, the suggestion is made that birth, despite its original absurdity, is just as fundamental to man as death. Paradoxically enough, O'Gorman is willing to concede everything to "Heidegger's genius" except the absurdity of not having left room in his thought for "the possibility of the absurd." That possibility is embodied in the immortal figure of Don Quixote, the eternal pursuer of the absurd. Thus the *Crisis and Future of Historical Science* closes with the idea that an adequate historicism must include man's pursuit of the absurd as an integral part of human existence. For the "absurd," by which O'Gorman means the "ideal," is as significant in human history as the "real." [60]

Carrying one step further O'Gorman's penetrating analysis of what he calls "the crisis of history" *as a science,* the remainder of the chapter will deal very briefly with what can be designated "the crisis of historicism" *as a philosophy* in present-day Mexico via an examination of Justino Fernández's work in contemporary Mexican painting. The latter's painstaking analysis of José Clemente Orozco in particular will point to this crisis in all its poignancy. Justino Fernández is, at the moment, doubtless the most thoroughgoing and sympathetic interpreter of that Mexican painter. What he has to say about Orozco's *arte vital* (the analogue of Ortega's *razón vital* in the realm of art) should be of the greatest philosophical import.[61]

Fernández is firmly convinced that the supreme characteristic of Mexico's contemporary mural painting is its "deliberate historicism." [62] Such *consciente historicismo* he takes as reflecting, however, the acute cultural crisis of our age, in which the traditional concept of absolute truth has been seriously challenged everywhere. Fernández maintains that of all the Mexican painters Orozco is the one who possesses the keenest sense of history. In fact, the painter himself has exclaimed with a touch of impatience: "A person who expects to grasp absolute truth in his hand would either be a fool or would have to remain forever mute." [63] Since the idea of man expressed throughout his paintings is that of a "complex entity" [64] shaped by the tragic forces of history, it follows that the only kind of truth we poor mortals can entertain is, perforce, "historical truth," a truth which is as "transitory" as human life itself. But—and this is the difference between the appraisals by Fernández and his close friend O'Gorman—such "conditioned truth" constitutes, in the former's opinion, "the sin of historicism." [65] Fernández, starting from the same epistemological premise as O'Gorman, arrives at an opposite conclusion regarding the value of historicism as a theory of truth. Thus, in the end, one man's epistemological food is another man's poison.

What, then, is *el pecado del historicismo* for Fernández? In a word, it is "pride," the most ancient of sins, born and bred in the celebrated Garden of Eden. For Fernández, perhaps the greatest error to which the "sin" of historicism has led is "conceiving the plurality of truth as inherent in human life." [66] Although the Mexican art critic, strangely enough, is fond of affiliating himself with Ortega's Madrid School, no more anti-Orteguian statement could have been uttered than the last one, given the perspectivist doctrine which defends the very plurality of truth. At any event, however inconsistent in epistemology, Fernández is the only neo-Orteguian in Mexico who already senses, dimly at least, that there is something wrong with the historicist conception of truth.

Orozco, as his friendly critic sees him, depicts in his paintings both the *relativización* which corrodes our present age and the way of saving ourselves from it. The ultimate message of his art, according to Fernández, is that man can somehow save himself through "consciousness of the trans-human," that is, through Something Unknowable beyond man. For there is a "metaphysical meaning" [67] pervading all his work, which, in reminding us of our intrinsic limitations as finite men, serves to emancipate us from human pride. This metaphysical factor, the source of the religious, is what gives man a sense of his proper place in the universe.

Fernández develops his thesis that Orozco is an "existentialist" painter by analyzing in detail the paintings themselves. Following the artist's own advice, he urges us to avoid the mistake made by the general public, who want to *hear* painting rather than *see* it. With Fernández as our guide, what is it we can learn on looking at those works with the aesthetic eye? Precisely what has been denominated "the crisis of historicism"—a crisis which is really a consequence of absolutizing each relative or conditioned truth. Furthermore, inasmuch as he generalizes to the effect that contemporary Mexican painting is an authentic "mirror" of the Mexican world—its Renaissance so to speak—the implication may be drawn, in closing, that the initial preoccupation of the neo-Orteguians with "the philosophy of Mexican culture" has now reached a critical stage in Mexico. For Orozco, in having manifested himself as a "citizen of the world," as Fernández calls him, has definitely gone beyond the narrow nationalistic frontiers of their relatively restricted type of *Nuevo Humanismo*. Despite his original allegiance to the ideology of the Mexican Revolution, his is a tragic "vision of humanity" [68] *as a whole,* not merely a vision of Mexico *à la* Ramos nor a vision of America *à la* Zea. Thus the significance of Orozco as a Mexican painter lies in his being a magnificent revealer of the tragic sense of life characteristic of the Latin-American soul.

Finally, as to which kind of humanism is going to prevail in the One World of the future, only history can tell. And history, like grapes, must wait till autumn to ripen. Meanwhile, whatever kind of humanistic faith may be in store for the future, the fact remains that Ortega's perspectivist ideas have been the greatest single intellectual force in the nationalization of the Mexican mind. The most recent evidence of the effect of these ideas on the current interest in *la mexicanidad* is the appearance of a new philosophical group in Mexico called Hiperión, the general concern of which is with what it describes as "the ontology of the Mexican man." The career of this existentialist group is too young to warrant analysis at present, but its place in the second half of twentieth-century Mexican thought will doubtless be the subject of a future historian of ideas in Mexico.

6

Chapter References

I

1. Gerald W. Johnson, *Our English Heritage* (N.Y.: J. B. Lippincott Co., 1949), p. 229.

2. Alfred N. Whitehead, *Science and the Modern World* (N.Y.: The Macmillan Co., 1925), p. 11.

3. F. S. C. Northrop, *The Meeting of East and West* (N.Y.: The Macmillan Co., 1946), p. x.

4. Frederick J. E. Woodbridge, "The Nature of Man," *Columbia University Quarterly,* Vol. XXIII (1931), 407.

5. José Vasconcelos and Manuel Gamio, *Aspects of Mexican Civilization* (Chicago: University of Chicago Press, 1926), p. 79.

6. Waldo Frank, "The Hispano-American's World," *The Nation,* Vol. 158 (1941), 616-617.

7. F. S. C. Northrop, *op. cit.,* pp. 15-65; *The Logic of the Sciences and the Humanities* (N.Y.: The Macmillan Co., 1947), pp. 334-335.

8. Aldous Huxley, "Ciudad de México," *Tierra Nueva,* Vol. II (1941), 169.

9. Francisco García Calderón, "Las corrientes filosóficas en la América Latina" (1908) in *Ideas e impresiones* (Madrid: Editorial América, 1919), p. 47.

10. Justino Fernández, *José Clemente Orozco: Forma e idea* (Mexico: Librería Porrúa, 1942), p. 65, p. 137.

11. Allan Nevins, in *The New York Times Book Review,* August 21, 1949, p. 17.

12. José Gaos, *Pensamiento de lengua española* (Mexico: Editorial Stylo, 1945), pp. 15-118; "Introduction," *Antología del pensamiento de lengua española en la edad contemporánea* (Mexico: Editorial Séneca, 1945).

II

1. F. S. C. Northrop, *The Logic of the Sciences and the Humanities,* p. 293, p. 344.

2. Bertrand Russell, *A History of Western Philosophy* (N.Y.: Simon and Schuster, Inc., 1945), pp. 596-597.

3. Risieri Frondizi, "Tendencies in Contemporary Latin-American Philosophy," in *Inter-American Intellectual Interchange* (Austin: University of Texas Press, 1943), pp. 35-48.

4. Herbert W. Schneider, *A History of American Philosophy* (N.Y.: Columbia University Press, 1946), p. viii.

5. Fray Alonso de la Vera Cruz, *Investigación filosófico-natural: Los libros del alma* (Libros I y II), trans. Oswaldo Robles (Mexico: Imprenta Universitaria, 1942), p. viii; Samuel Ramos, *Historia de la filosofía en México* (Mexico: Imprenta Universitaria, 1943), pp. 28-30; José Almoina, "El erasmismo de Zumárraga," *Filosofía y Letras,* Vol. XV (1948), 93-126.

6. Quoted in Augustín Yáñez, *Fichas mexicanas* (Mexico: El Colegio de México, 1945), p. 52.

7. Edmundo O'Gorman, *Fundamentos de la historia de América* (Mexico: Imprenta Universitaria, 1942), p. 46, p. 61.

8. Quoted in Emeterio Valverde Téllez, *Bibliografía filosófica mexicana,* Vol. I (2nd ed.; León, 1913), p. 109.

9. Quoted in Samuel Ramos, *op. cit.,* p. 80. Cf. Antonio Caso, "Don Juan Benito Díaz de Gamarra, un filósofo mexicano discípulo de Descartes," *Revista de Literatura Mexicana,* Vol. I (1940), 197-213.

10. John Tate Lanning, *Academic Culture in the Spanish Colonies* (N.Y.: Oxford University Press, 1940), pp. 87-88.

11. Carl L. Becker, *The Heavenly City of the Eighteenth-Century Philosophers* (New Haven, Conn.: Yale University Press, 1932), p. 29.

12. Antonio Gibaja y Patrón, *Comentario crítico, histórico, auténtico a las revoluciones sociales de México,* Vol. I (Mexico: Tipografía Universal, 1926), p. 525.

13. Juan Hernández Luna, "Las raíces ideológicas de Hidalgo y nuestra Revolución de Independencia," *Filosofía y Letras,* Vol. XV (1948), 77.

14. Samuel Ramos, *op. cit.,* p. 104.

15. José Gaos, "Introduction," *Antología del pensamiento de lengua española en la edad contemporánea.*

16. Secretaría de Educación Pública de México, *Documentos de la Guerra de Independencia* (Mexico: Ediciones de la Secretaría de Educación Pública, 1945), pp. 48-49.

17. Leopoldo Zea, *Dos etapas del pensamiento en Hispanoamérica: Del romanticismo al positivismo* (Mexico: El Colegio de México, 1949), pp. 30-43.

18. Quoted in Leopoldo Zea, "Positivism and Porfirism in Latin America," trans. Helene Weyl, in F. S. C. Northrop (ed.), *Ideological Differences and World Order* (New Haven, Conn.: Yale University Press, 1949), p. 176.

19. *Ibid.,* pp. 166-191; *El positivismo en México,* Vol. I (Mexico: El Colegio de México, 1943), p. 38; *Apogeo y decadencia del positivismo en México,* Vol. II (Mexico: El Colegio de México, 1944), p. 93.

20. Emeterio Valverde Téllez, *op. cit.*, Vol. II, p. 9.

21. Gabino Barreda, *Estudios,* José Fuentes Mares (ed.) (Mexico: Universidad Nacional Autónoma, 1941), pp. 71-110.

22. J. Joaquín Izquierdo, *Claudio Bernard* (Mexico: Cultura, 1943), p. 22.

23. Leopoldo Zea, *vide* no. 18, pp. 180-181.

24. *Ibid.*, p. 174.

25. *Loc. cit.*

26. Leopoldo Zea, *Apogeo y decadencia del positivismo en México,* Vol. II, pp. 114-118, pp. 159-175.

27. José Ortega y Gasset, *The Modern Theme,* trans. James Cleugh (N.Y.: W. W. Norton and Co., 1933), pp. 86-96.

28. José Vasconcelos *et al., Conferencias del Ateneo de la Juventud* (Mexico: Imprenta Lacaud, 1910), p. 164.

29. Pedro Henríquez Ureña, "La cultura de las humanidades," *Revista Bimestre Cubana,* Vol. IX (1914), 241-252.

30. Quoted in Alfonso Reyes, *Pasado inmediato y otros ensayos* (Mexico: El Colegio de México, 1941), p. 47.

31. Antonio Caso, *México: Apuntamientos de cultura patria* (Mexico: Imprenta Universitaria, 1943), pp. 91-94.

32. Justo Sierra, *Prosas,* Antonio Caso (ed.) (Mexico: Universidad Nacional Autónoma, 1939), pp. 158-173.

33. Pedro Henríquez Ureña, *Seis ensayos en busca de nuestra expresión* (Buenos Aires: Babel, 1928), p. 14.

34. *Ibid., Horas de estudio* (Paris: P. Ollendorff, 1910), p. 13.

35. José Vasconcelos, *Ulises Criollo* (4th ed.; Mexico: Ediciones Botas, 1935), p. 467.

36. *Ibid.*, p. 464.

37. *Ibid.*, p. 465.

38. Ezequiel A. Chávez, *Dios, el universo y la libertad* (Barcelona: Araluce, 1935), pp. 16-17.

III

1. Antonio Caso, *La existencia como economía, como desinterés y como caridad* (3rd ed.; Mexico: Secretaría de Educación Pública, 1943), p. 13.

2. ——————., *Problemas filosóficos* (Mexico: Librería Porrúa, 1915), pp. 205-206.

3. ——————., *La existencia como economía, como desinterés y como caridad* (2nd ed., Mexico, México Moderno, 1919), p. 76.

4. ——————., *El concepto de la historia universal y la filosofía de los valores* (2nd ed.; Mexico: Ediciones Botas, 1933), pp. 81-84.

5. ——————., *Samuel Ramos y yo: Un ensayo de valoración personal* (Mexico, 1927), p. 11.

6. ——————., *Ensayos críticos y polémicos* (Mexico: México Moderno, 1922), pp. 73-76.

7. Henri Bergson, *The Two Sources of Morality and Religion,* trans. R. A. Audra and C. Brereton (N.Y.: Henry Holt and Co., 1935), p. 245, p. 87, p. 240, pp. 236-239, p. 209, p. 91; *Creative Evolution,* trans. Arthur Mitchell (N.Y.: Henry Holt and Co., 1911), p. 248.

8. Antonio Caso, *La existencia. . .* (2nd ed., 1919), p. 128.

9. ——————., *La existencia. . .* (3rd ed., 1943), p. 21.

10. *Ibid.,* p. 18.

11. Antonio Caso, *La persona humana y el estado totalitario* (Mexico: Universidad Nacional Autónoma, 1941), p. 191.

12. ——————., *La filosofía de la cultura y el materialismo histórico* (Mexico: Alba, 1936), p. 160.

13. ——————., *La existencia. . .* (3rd ed., 1943), p. 33.

14. *Ibid.,* p. 35.

15. Henri Bergson, *Creative Evolution,* p. 129.

16. Antonio Caso, *La existencia. . .* (3rd ed., 1943), p. 44.

17. *Ibid.,* p. 75.

18. *Ibid.,* p. 87.

19. Antonio Caso, *La filosofía de la cultura. . .*, p. 59.

20. Henri Bergson, *Creative Evolution*, p. 159.

21. Antonio Caso, *La existencia. . .* (3rd ed., 1943), p. 82.

22. *Ibid.*, pp. 77-78.

23. *Ibid.*, p. 185.

24. *Ibid.*, p. 179.

25. *Ibid.*, p. 127.

26. *Ibid.*, p. 137, p. 164.

27. *Ibid.*, p. 154.

28. Antonio Caso, *El concepto de la historia universal. . .*, p. 119.

29. —————., *La existencia. . .* (3rd ed., 1943), p. 160.

30. *Ibid.*, p. 160.

31. *Ibid.*, pp. 164-165.

32. *Ibid.*, p. 181.

33. *Ibid.*, p. 187, p. 163.

34. *Ibid.*, pp. 181-187.

35. M. F. Ashley Montagu, "The Origin and Nature of Social Life and the Biological Basis of Cooperation," *The Journal of Social Psychology*, Vol. 29 (1949), 267-283.

36. Antonio Caso, *La existencia. . .* (2nd ed., 1919), p. 17, p. 113; (3rd ed., 1943), p. 155.

IV

1. José Vasconcelos, *Ulises criollo* (4th ed.; Mexico: Ediciones Botas, 1935); *La tormenta* (3rd ed.; Mexico: Ediciones Botas, 1936); *El desastre* (Mexico: Ediciones Botas, 1938); *El proconsulado* (2nd ed.; Mexico: Ediciones Botas, 1939).

2. —————., *Indología: Una interpretación de la cultura ibero-americana.* (Barcelona: Agencia Mundial de Librería, 1927), p. xxv.

3. G. F. MacGregor (ed.), *Vasconcelos* (Mexico: Ediciones de la Secretaría de Educación Pública, 1942), pp. 3-51.

4. ——————., "Bergson en México," *Filosofía y Letras,* Vol. 1 (1941), 239.

5. Henri Bergson, *The Two Sources of Morality and Religion,* p. 104, p. 245.

6. José Vasconcelos, *Tratado de metafísica* (Mexico: México Joven, 1929), p. 86, p. 95, p. 205.

7. ——————., "Teoría dinámica del derecho," *Revista Positiva,* Vol. VI (1907), 1-24.

8. ——————., *Lógica orgánica* (Mexico: El Colegio Nacional, 1945), p. xxxvii; A. N. Whitehead, *Adventures of Ideas* (N.Y.: The Macmillan Co., 1933), p. 191.

9. ——————., *Pitágoras: Una teoría del ritmo* (Mexico: Cultura, 1921), p. 73.

10. W. P. Montague, *The Ways of Things* (N.Y.: Prentice-Hall, Inc., 1940), pp. 482-510.

11. José Vasconcelos, *El monismo estético* (Mexico: Cultura, 1918), pp. 101-104.

12. ——————., *La revulsión de la energía* (Mexico, 1924), pp. 1-22.

13. ——————., *Estética* (3rd ed., Mexico: Ediciones Botas, 1945), p. 418, p. 283; *Etica* (2nd ed., Mexico: Ediciones Botas, 1939), p. 506, p. 395.

14. ——————., *Estética,* p. 47.

15. ——————., *El realismo científico* (Mexico: Centro de Estudios Filosóficos, 1943), *passim.*

16. ——————., *Estética,* p. 170, p. 418.

17. ——————., *Tratado de metafísica,* pp. 163ff.; *Estética,* p. 34; *Lógica orgánica,* p. 28.

18. ——————., *Estética,* p. 86.

19. *Ibid.,* p. 36; *Tratado de metafísica,* p. 221.

20. ——————., *Tratado de metafísica,* p. 328.

21. *Ibid.,* p. 219.

22. W. P. Montague, *The Ways of Things,* pp. 418-439.

23. José Vasconcelos, *Tratado de metafísica,* p. 181, p. 190, p. 213.

24. —————., *Estética,* p. 32, p. 92.

25. —————., *Etica,* p. 271.

26. —————., *Historia del pensamiento filosófico* (Mexico: Universidad Nacional, 1937), p. 527.

27. —————., *Tratado de metafísica,* pp. 105-173.

28. *Ibid.,* p. 343.

29. —————., *Lógica orgánica,* p. liii, *passim.*

30. *Ibid.,* p. 150.

31. —————., *Etica,* p. 85.

32. —————., *Estética,* p. 102.

33. —————., "Desarrollo estético de la creación," in *Papers and Abstracts of the Second Inter-American Congress of Philosophy* (N.Y.: Columbia University Press, 1947), p. 129. Parallel English trans. E. Vivas, "The Aesthetic Development of Creation," p. 128.

34. *Ibid.,* p. 124.

35. José Vasconcelos, *Estética,* p. 351.

36. *Ibid.,* p. 215, p. 641; "Dessarrolo estético de la creación," p. 127.

37. B. Croce, *Breviario de estética,* trans. S. Ramos (Mexico: Cultura, 1925), p. 84; Henri Bergson, *Laughter,* trans. C. Brereton and F. Rothwell (N.Y.: The Macmillan Co., 1911), pp. 150-163, esp. p. 157; J. Vasconcelos, *Estética,* p. 593.

38. Henri Bergson, *The Creative Mind,* trans. M. L. Andison (N.Y.: Philosophical Library, 1946), pp. 162-163, pp. 185-186.

39. José Vasconcelos, *Estética,* p. 61.

40. —————., *Etica,* p. 313.

41. —————., *Tratado de metafísica,* p. 270; *Etica,* p. 455.

42. —————., *Etica,* pp. 152-153.

43. *Ibid., passim.*

44. —————., *Aspects of Mexican Civilization,* p. 21.

45. —————., *Historia del pensamiento filosófico,* pp. 525-531.

46. G. F. MacGregor (ed.), *op. cit.,* p. 135.

47. John Dewey, *Art as Experience* (N.Y.: Minton, Balch and Co., 1934), p. 6.

48. José Vasconcelos, *Tratado de metafísica,* p. 198.

49.——————., *Estética,* p. 123; G. F. MacGregor (ed.), *op. cit.,* p. 142.

V

1. Samuel Ramos, *Historia de la filosofía en México,* p. 149.

2. José Romano Muñoz, "Ni irracionalismo ni racionalismo, sino filosofía crítica," *Ulises,* Vol. I (1927), 4-10.

3. Oswaldo Robles, "Ensayo de una metafísica existencial agustino-tomista," *Revista Universitaria,* Universidad Autónoma de Guadalajara, (1943), 75-79.

4. José Fuentes Mares, *Kant y la evolución de la conciencia socio-política moderna* (Mexico: Editorial Stylo, 1946), p. 13.

5. José Ortega y Gasset, *Concord and Liberty,* trans. H. Weyl (N.Y.: W. W. Norton and Co., 1946), p. 137.

6. Nicholas J. Spykman, *The Social Theory of Georg Simmel* (Chicago: The University of Chicago Press, 1925), p. 4.

7. José Ortega y Gasset, *The Modern Theme,* pp. 39-40.

8. Werner Brock, *An Introduction to Contemporary German Philosophy* (Cambridge, England: The University Press, 1935), p. 70.

9. José Ortega y Gasset, *Meditaciones del Quijote* (2nd ed.; Madrid: Calpe, 1921), p. 35.

10. ——————., *Toward a Philosophy of History,* trans. H. Weyl (N.Y.: W. W. Norton and Co., 1941), pp. 202-204.

11. ——————., *The Modern Theme,* p. 86.

12. ——————., *Mission of the University,* trans. H. L. Nostrand (Princeton: Princeton University Press, 1944), p. 15.

13. ——————., *Toward a Philosophy of History,* p. 216.

14. ——————., *Concord and Liberty,* pp. 141-142.

15. ———., *Mission of the University*, p. 89.

16. Nicola Abbagnano, *Introduzione all'esistenzialismo* (2nd ed.; Turin: Taylor Editore, 1947); Annibale Pastore, *La volontà dell'assurdo: Storia e crisi dell'esistenzialismo* (Milan: Edizioni Giovanni Bolla, 1948).

17. José Ortega y Gasset, *Tríptico* (Buenos Aires, Espasa-Calpe Argentina, 1941), pp. 130-132.

18. ———., *Toward a Philosophy of History*, p. 21.

19. *Ibid.*, p. 14, p. 18.

20. ———., *El tema de nuestro tiempo* (3rd ed.; Buenos Aires: Espasa-Calpe Argentina, 1941), p. 83.

21. ———., *Toward a Philosophy of History*, p. 24.

22. *Ibid.*, p. 100.

23. ———., *Tríptico*, p. 132.

24. ———., *Concord and Liberty*, p. 164.

25. ———., *The Modern Theme*, p. 90.

26. *Ibid.*, pp. 88-92.

27. ———., *Tríptico*, p. 113.

28. ———., *Concord and Liberty*, p. 13.

29. Samuel Ramos, *Historia de la filosofía en México*, p. 153.

30. ———., *Hipótesis* (Mexico: Ediciones de "Ulises," 1928), pp. 115-123.

31. *Ibid.*, *Historia de la filosofía en México*, p. 147; *Veinte años de educación en México* (Mexico; Imprenta Universitaria, 1941), p. 23.

32. José Ortega y Gasset, *The Modern Theme*, p. 144.

33. Samuel Ramos, *El perfil del hombre y la cultura en México* (2nd ed.; Mexico: P. Robredo, 1938), p. 73, p. 155.

34. *Ibid.*, p. 140, p. 167, p. 179.

35. Samuel Ramos, *Más allá de la moral de Kant* (Mexico: Chapero, 1938), p. 19, p. 28; *Hacia un nuevo humanismo* (Mexico: La Casa de España en México, 1940), p. 16, p. 32, p. 34, pp. 45-63, p. 79, p. 149.

36. Leopoldo Zea, *Ensayos sobre filosofía en la historia* (Mexico: Editorial Stylo, 1948), p. 144.

37. José Ortega y Gasset, *Toward a Philosophy of History*, pp. 43-83; Leopoldo Zea, *Ensayos sobre filosofía en la historia*, pp. 178-188.

38. Leopoldo Zea, *op. cit.*, p. 180.

39. *Ibid.*, pp. 189-198.

40. Leopoldo Zea, *En torno a una filosofía americana* (Mexico: El Colegio de México, 1945), p. 15.

41. *Ibid.*, p. 22.

42. José Ortega y Gasset, *Toward a Philosophy of History*, pp. 87-161.

43. *Ibid.*, p. 16.

44. Leopoldo Zea, *En torno a una filosofía americana*, pp. 25-27.

45. *Ibid.*, p. 32.

46. *Ibid.*, pp. 30-31.

47. *Ibid.*, pp. 45-47.

48. *Ibid.*, pp. 52-53.

49. *Ibid.*, p. 56.

50. *Ibid.*, p. 67.

51. *Ibid.*, p. 66.

52. Edmundo O'Gorman, *Fundamentos de la historia de América*, p. xiv.

53. *Ibid.*, p. 90.

54. *Ibid.*, p. 106.

55. Edmundo O'Gorman, *Crisis y porvenir de la ciencia histórica* (Mexico: Imprenta Universitaria, 1947), p. xi, p. 188, p. 204.

56. *Ibid.*, p. 57, pp. 108-114, p. 149, 171, pp. 190-202, p. 306.

57. *Ibid.*, p. 113, p. 203, p. 210, p. 246, p. 270.

58. *Ibid.*, pp. 286-287; Morris R. Cohen, *The Meaning of Human History* (La Salle, Ill.: Open Court Publishing Co., 1947), p. 42.

59. Edmundo O'Gorman, *Crisis y porvenir de la ciencia histórica*, p. 285.

60. *Ibid.*, pp. 203-222, p. 282, pp. 289-294, pp. 303-305, pp. 323-330.

61. Justino Fernández, *José Clemente Orozco: Forma e idea*, p. 155.

62. —————., *Rufino Tamayo* (Mexico: Imprenta Universitaria, 1948), p. 39.
63. Quoted in Justino Fernández, *José Clemente Orozco: Forma e idea*, p. 33.
64. *Ibid.*, p. 127.
65. *Ibid.*, p. 33, p. 153.
66. *Ibid.*, p. 156.
67. Justino Fernández, *Prometeo: Ensayo sobre pintura contemporánea* (Mexico: Editorial Porrúa, 1945), p. 7.
68. —————., *José Clemente Orozco: Forma e idea*, p. 29.

A SELECTED BIBLIOGRAPHY

OF

RECENT MEXICAN THOUGHT

AHUMADA, HERMINIO, JR. *José Vasconcelos*. Mexico: Ediciones Botas, 1937.

AMERICAN PHILOSOPHICAL ASSOCIATION. "Papers and Discussions of the First Inter-American Conference of Philosophy," *Philosophy and Phenomenological Research*, IV (1943), 127-233.

"Papers and Abstracts of the Second Inter-American Congress of Philosophy," *Ibid.*, IX (1949), 345-626.

ARAGÓN, AGUSTÍN. *Essai sur l'histoire du positivisme au Mexique*. Paris: Societé Positiviste, 1898.

ASOCIACIÓN METODÓFILA. *Gabino Barreda: Anales*. Mexico, 1877.

ATENEO DE LA JUVENTUD. *Conferencias*. Mexico: Imprenta Lacaud, 1910.

BARREDA, GABINO. *Estudios*, José Fuentes Mares (ed.). Mexico: Universidad Nacional Autónoma, 1941.

BELGODERE, FRANCISCO JAVIER A. *La verdad, la ciencia y la filosofía*. Mexico, 1939.

CABRERA MACÍA, MANUEL. *Bases para una fundamentación de la sociología*. Mexico, 1938.

Caso, Antonio. *La filosofía de la intuición.* Mexico: Edición de "Nosotros," 1914.

Problemas filosóficos, Mexico: Libreria Porrúa, 1915.

Filósofos y doctrinas morales, Mexico: Librería Porrúa, 1915.

La existencia como economía y como caridad: Ensayo sobre la esencia del cristianismo, Mexico: Porrúa Hnos., 1916; 2nd ed., *La existencia como economía, como desinterés y como caridad.* Mexico: México Moderno, 1919; 3rd ed., Mexico: Secretaría de Educación Pública, 1943.

La filosofía francesa contemporánea. Mexico, 1917.

Discursos a la nación mexicana. Mexico: Librería Porrúa, 1922.

Ensayos críticos y polémicos, Mexico: México Moderno, 1922.

El concepto de la historia universal. Mexico: México Moderno, 1923; 2nd ed., *El concepto de la historia universal y la filosofía de los valores.* Mexico: Ediciones Botas, 1933.

Doctrinas e ideas. Mexico: Herrero, 1924.

El problema de México y la ideología nacional. Mexico: Cultura, 1924.

Principios de estética. 1st ed., Mexico: Publicaciones de la Secretaría de Educación, 1925; 2nd ed., Mexico: Editorial Porrúa, 1944.

Historia y antología del pensamiento filosófico. Mexico: Franco-Americana, 1926.

Sociología genética y sistemática. 1st ed., Secretaría de Educación Pública, 1927; 5th ed., Mexico: Editorial Porrúa, 1948.

Samuel Ramos y yo: Un ensayo de valoración personal. Mexico, 1927.

El acto ideatorio. Mexico: Librería Porrúa, 1934.

La filosofía de Husserl. Mexico: Imprenta Mundial, 1934.

Nuevos discursos a la nación mexicana. Mexico: P. Robredo, 1934.

La filosofía de la cultura y el materialismo histórico. Mexico: Alba, 1936.

Myerson y la física moderna. Mexico: La Casa de España en México, 1939.

La persona humana y el estado totalitario. Mexico: Universidad Nacional Autónoma, 1941.

Positivismo, neo-positivismo y fenomenología. Mexico: Compañía General Editora, 1941.

El peligro del hombre. Mexico: Editorial Stylo, 1942.

Filósofos y moralistas franceses. Mexico: Editorial Stylo, 1943.

México: Apuntamientos de cultura patria. Mexico: Imprenta Universitaria, 1943.

(and Guillermo Héctor Rodríguez). *Ensayos polémicos sobre la escuela filosófica de Marburgo.* Mexico, 1945.

CENTRO DE ESTUDIOS FILOSÓFICOS. *Homenaje a Bergson.* Mexico: Imprenta Universitaria, 1941.

Homenaje a Antonio Caso. Mexico: Editorial Stylo, 1947.

CEVALLOS, MIGUEL ANGEL. *Estancias espirituales.* Mexico, 1936.

(and Francisco Larroyo). *La lógica de la ciencia.* 1st ed., Mexico: Librería Porrúa, 1938; 6th ed., *ibid.,* 1948.

Ensayo sobre el conocimiento. Mexico: Antigua Librería Robredo, 1944.

CHÁVEZ, EZEQUIEL A. *Dios, el universo y la libertad.* Barcelona: Araluce, 1935.

Masaryk como filósofo. Mexico: Universidad Nacional, 1938.

Anhelo de infinito y ansia de eternidad, Mexico: Editorial de Silva, 1942.

De dónde venimos y a dónde vamos? Mexico: El Colegio Nacional, 1946.

COSÍO VILLEGAS, DANIEL. *Extremos de América.* Mexico: Tezontle, 1949.

CRAWFORD, WILLIAM REX. *A Century of Latin-American Thought.* Cambridge: Harvard University Press, 1944, pp. 247-294.

DEÚSTUA, ALEJANDRO OCTAVIO. *La estética de José Vasconcelos.* Lima: Taller Gráfico de P. Barrantes, 1939.

FERNÁNDEZ, JUSTINO. *José Clemente Orozco: Forma e idea.* Mexico: Librería Porrúa, 1942.

201

Prometeo: Ensayo sobre pintura contemporánea. Mexico: Editorial Porrúa, 1945.

Rufino Tamayo. Mexico: Imprenta Universitaria, 1948.

FRONDIZI, RISIERI. *Panorama de la filosofía latinoamericana contemporánea.* Buenos Aires: Cuaderno Minerva, 1944.

FUENTES MARES, JOSÉ. *Ley, sociedad y política.* Mexico: Imprenta Universitaria, 1943.

Kant y la evolución de la conciencia socio-política moderna. Mexico: Editorial Stylo, 1946.

GALLEGOS, ROCAFULL, JOSÉ M. *El pensamiento mexicano en los siglos XVI y XVII.* Mexico: Centro de Estudios Filosóficos, 1951.

GAOS, JOSÉ (AND FRANCISCO LARROYO). *Dos ideas de la filosofía.* Mexico: La Casa de España en México, 1940.

El pensamiento hispanoamericano. Mexico: El Colegio de México, n. d.

Antología del pensamiento de lengua española en la edad contemporánea, Mexico: Editorial Séneca, 1945.

Pensamiento de lengua española. Mexico: Editorial Stylo, 1945.

GARCÍA MÁYNEZ, EDUARDO. *El problema filosófico-jurídico de la validez del derecho.* Mexico: Imprenta Mundial, 1935.

El derecho natural en la época de Sócrates. Mexico, 1939.

Libertad como derecho y como poder. Mexico: Compañía General Editora, 1941.

Una discusión sobre el concepto jurídico de la libertad (Respuesta a Carlos Cossio). Mexico: Imprenta Universitaria, 1942.

Etica. 1st ed., Mexico: Centro de Estudios Filosóficos, 1944; 2nd ed., Mexico: Editorial Porrúa, 1949.

La definición del derecho: Ensayo de perspectivismo jurídico. Mexico: Editorial Stylo, 1948.

Latin-American Legal Philosophy, Cambridge: Harvard University Press, 1948, pp. 459-547.

GÓMEZ ROBLEDO, ANTONIO. *Política de Vitoria.* Mexico: Universidad Nacional Autónoma, 1940.

Cristianismo y filosofía en la experiencia agustiniana. Mexico, 1942.

La filosofía en el Brasil. Mexico: Imprenta Universitaria, 1946.

GONZÁLEZ CASANOVA, PABLO. *El misoneísmo y la modernidad cristiana en el siglo XVIII.* Mexico: El Colegio de México, 1948.

GONZÁLEZ y GONZÁLEZ, LUIS. *El optimismo nacionalista como factor de la independencia de México.* Mexico: El Colegio de México, 1948.

HENRÍQUEZ UREÑA, PEDRO. *Horas de estudio.* Paris: P. Ollendorff, 1910.

Seis ensayos en busca de nuestra expresión. Buenos Aires: Babel, 1928.

HERNÁNDEZ CHÁVEZ, JOSÉ. *Lógica.* Mexico: Editorial Jus, 1946.

HERNÁNDEZ LUNA, JUAN. *José Antonio Alzate.* Mexico: Secretaría de Educàción Pública, 1945.

INSTITUTE OF LATIN-AMERICAN STUDIES. *Inter-American Intellectual Interchange.* Austin: University of Texas Press, 1943; *Intellectual Trends in Latin America, ibid.,* 1945.

INSÚA RODRÍGUEZ, RAMÓN. *Historia de la filosofía en Hispano-América.* Guayaquil: Imprenta de la Universidad, 1945.

IZQUIERDO, JOAQUÍN J. *Claudio Bernard.* Mexico: Cultura, 1943.

LANNING, JOHN TATE. *Academic Culture in the Spanish Colonies.* New York: Oxford University Press, 1940.

LARROYO, FRANCISCO. *La filosofía de los valores.* Mexico: Logos, 1936.

Los principios de la ética social, 1st ed., Mexico: Librería Porrúa, 1936; 6th ed., *ibid.,* 1946.

Bibliografía general del socialismo. Mexico: Logos, 1937.

Bases para una teoría dinámica de las ciencias. Mexico: Pallas, 1941.

Exposición y crítica del personalismo espiritualista de nuestro tiempo: Misiva a Francisco Romero. Mexico: Logos, 1941.

El romanticismo filosófico: Observaciones a la Weltanschauung de Joaquín Xirau. Mexico: Logos, 1941.

Historia general de la pedagogía. Mexico: Editorial Porrúa, 1946.

Historia de la filosofía en Norte-América. Mexico: Editorial Stylo, 1946.

Historia comparada de la educación en México. 1st ed., Mexico: Editorial Porrúa, 1946; 2nd ed., *ibid.,* 1948.

El existencialismo: Sus fuentes y direcciones. Mexico: Editorial Porrúa, 1951.

LOMBARDO TOLEDANO, VICENTE. *El derecho público y las nuevas corrientes filosóficas.* Mexico, 1919.

Etica. Mexico; México Moderno, 1922.

Escritos filosóficos. Mexico: México Nuevo, 1937.

MAYAGOITIA, DAVID. *Ambiente filosófico de la Nueva España.* Mexico: Editorial Jus, 1945.

MÉNDEZ PLANCARTE, GABRIEL. *Hidalgo: Reformador intelectual.* Mexico: Letras de México, 1945.

MENÉNDEZ SAMARÁ, ADOLFO. *La estética y sus relaciones: Ensayo de historia.* Mexico, 1937.

La estética y su método dialéctico: El valor de lo bello. Mexico: Letras de México, 1937.

Dos ensayos sobre Heidegger. Mexico: Letras de México. 1939.

Fanatismo y misticismo. Mexico: La Casa de España en México, 1940.

Breviario de psicología. 1st ed., Mexico: Librería Porrúa, 1941; 2nd ed., *ibid.,* 1945.

Iniciación en la filosofía. Mexico: Librería Porrúa, 1943.

Menester y precisión del ser. Mexico: Antigua Librería Robredo, 1946.

MORA, JOSÉ MARÍA LUIS. *Ensayos, ideas, y retratos.* Arturo Arnáiz y Freg (ed.). Mexico: Universidad Nacional Autónoma, 1941.

México y sus revoluciones, 3 vols. Mexico: Editorial Porrúa, 1950.

NAVARRO, BERNABÉ. *La introducción de la filosofía moderna en México.* Mexico: El Colegio de México, 1948.

NORTHROP, F. S. C. *The Meeting of East and West.* New York: The Macmillan Co., 1946, pp. 15-65.

Ideological Differences and World Order (ed.). New Haven, Conn.: Yale University Press, 1949, pp. 166-191.

O'GORMAN, EDMUNDO. *Fundamentos de la historia de América.* Mexico: Imprenta Universitaria, 1942.

Crisis y porvenir de la ciencia histórica. Mexico: Imprenta Universitaria, 1947.

La idea del descubrimiento de América. Mexico: Centro de Estudios Filosóficos, 1951.

PÉREZ MARCHAND, MONELISA LINA. *A Critical Study of Some Currents of Contemporary Philosophical Thought in Latin America.* Baltimore, 1940.

Dos etapas ideológicas del siglo XVIII en México. Mexico: Fondo de Cultura Económica, 1945.

PORTUGAL, JOSÉ M. DE JESÚS. *El positivismo: Su historia y sus errores.* Barcelona, 1908.

PRECIADO HERNÁNDEZ, RAFAEL. *Lecciones de filosofía del derecho.* Mexico: Editorial Jus, 1947.

QUIROZ MARTÍNEZ, OLGA VICTORIA. *La introducción de la filosofía moderna en España.* Mexico: El Colegio de México, 1949.

RAMOS, SAMUEL. *Hipótesis.* Mexico: Ediciones de "Ulises," 1928.

El perfil del hombre y la cultura en México. 1st ed., Mexico: Imprenta Mundial, 1934; 2nd ed., Mexico: P. Robredo, 1938.

Más allá de la moral de Kant. Mexico: Chapero, 1938.

Hacia un nuevo humanismo. Mexico: La Casa de España en México, 1940.

Veinte años de educación en México. Mexico: Imprenta Universitaria, 1941.

Historia de la filosofía en México. Mexico: Imprenta Universitaria, 1943.

Filosofía de la vida artística. Buenos Aires: Espasa-Calpe Argentina, 1950.

Reyes, Alfonso. *Cuestiones estéticas.* Paris: P. Ollendorff, 1911.

La crítica en la edad ateniense. Mexico: El Colegio de México, 1941.

Pasado inmediato y otros ensayos. Mexico: El Colegio de México, 1941.

Ultima Tule. Mexico: Ediciones de la Universidad Nacional Autónoma de México, 1942.

La antigua retórica. Mexico: Fondo de Cultura Económica, 1942.

La experiencia literaria. Buenos Aires: Editorial Losada, 1942.

El deslinde: Prolegómenos a la teoría literaria. Mexico: El Colegio de México, 1944.

The Position of America and Other Essays, trans., Harriet de Onís. New York: Knopf, 1950.

Rivera, Agustín. *La filosofía en la Nueva España.* Mexico: Logos, 1885.

Robles, Oswaldo. *El alma y el cuerpo.* Mexico: Veritas, 1935.

La teoría de la idea en Malebranche y en la tradición filosófica. Mexico: Veritas, 1937.

Esquema de antropología filosófica. Mexico: Pax, 1942.

Propedéutica filosófica. Mexico: Librería Porrúa, 1943; English trans., by Kurt F. Reinhardt, *The Main Problems of Philosophy,* Milwaukee: Bruce Publishing Co., 1946.

Introducción a la psicología científica. Mexico: Editorial Porrúa, 1948.

Filósofos mexicanos del siglo XVI. Mexico: Librería Porrúa, 1950.

Rodríguez, Guillermo Héctor. *El ideal de justicia y nuestro derecho positivo.* Mexico, 1934.

El metafisicismo de Kelsen. Mexico, 1947.

Etica y jurisprudencia. Mexico, 1947.

Romano Muñoz, José. *El secreto del bien y del mal: Etica valorativa.* 1st ed., Mexico: Antigua Librería Robredo, 1938; 3rd ed., *ibid.,* 1946.

Sánchez Villaseñor, José. *El sistema filosófico de Vasconcelos.* Mexico: Editorial Polis, 1939.

Pensamiento y trayectoria de José Ortega y Gasset. Mexico: Editorial Jus, 1943; English trans., by Joseph Small, *Ortega y Gasset, Existentialist.* Chicago: Regnery, 1949.

La crisis del historicismo y otros ensayos. Mexico: Editorial Jus, 1945.

Sesto, Julio. *Historia del pensamiento mexicano.* Vol. I. Mexico, 1942.

Sierra, Justo. *Prosas,* Antonio Caso (ed.). Mexico: Universidad Nacional Autónoma, 1939.

Evolución política del pueblo mexicano. Mexico: La Casa de España en México, 1940.

Sociedad Cubana de Filosofía. *El Tercer Congreso Interamericano de Filosofía.* Havana, 1950.

Valverde Téllez, Emeterio. *Apuntaciones sobre la filosofía en México.* Mexico, 1897.

Bibliografía filosófica mexicana. 2 Vols. 1st ed., León, 1907; 2nd ed., *ibid.,* 1913.

Vasconcelos, José. *Pitágoras: Una teoría del ritmo.* 1st ed., Havana, 1916; 2nd ed., Mexico: Cultura, 1921.

El monismo estético. Mexico: Cultura, 1918.

Estudios indostánicos. 1st ed., Mexico: México Moderno, 1920; 3rd ed., Mexico: Ediciones Botas, 1938.

La revulsión de la energía. Mexico, 1924.

La raza cósmica: Misión de la raza iberoamericana. Paris: Agencia Mundial de Librería, 1925.

(and Manuel Gamio). *Aspects of Mexican Civilization.* Chicago: University of Chicago Press, 1926.

Indología: Una interpretación de la cultura ibero-americana. Barcelona: Agencia Mundial de Librería, 1927.

Tratado de metafísica. Mexico: Editorial "México Joven," 1929.

Pesimismo alegre. Madrid: M. Aguilar, 1931.

Etica, 1st ed., Madrid: M. Aguilar, 1932; 2nd ed., Mexico: Ediciones Botas, 1939.

La cultura en Hispanoamérica. La Plata, 1934.

De Robinsón a Odiseo: Pedagogía estructurativa. Madrid: M. Aguilar, 1935.

Bolivarismo y monroísmo: Temas iberoamericanos. 1st ed., Santiago, Chile: Editorial Ercilla, 1935; 3rd ed., *ibid.,* 1937.

Estética. 1st ed., Mexico: Ediciones Botas, 1936; 3rd ed., *ibid.,* 1945.

Qué es el comunismo. Mexico: Ediciones Botas, 1936.

Historia del pensamiento filosófico. Mexico: Universidad Nacional, 1937.

Qué es la revolución. Mexico: Ediciones Botas, 1937.

Manual de filosofía. Mexico: Ediciones Botas, 1940.

El realismo científico. Mexico: Centro de Estudios Filosóficos, 1943.

Lógica orgánica. Mexico. El Colegio Nacional, 1945.

VILLORO, LUIS. *Los grandes momentos del indigenismo en México.* Mexico: El Colegio de México, 1950.

YAMUNI TABUSH, VERA. *Conceptos e imágenes en pensadores de lengua española.* Mexico: El Colegio de México, 1951.

YÁÑEZ, AGUSTÍN. *El contenido social de la literatura iberoamericana.* Mexico: El Colegio de México, n.d.

Fichas mexicanas. Mexico: El Colegio de México, 1945.

ZAVALA, SILVIO. *Filosofía de la Conquista.* Mexico: Fondo de Cultura Económica, 1947.

ZEA, LEOPOLDO. *El positivismo en México,* Vol. I. Mexico: El Colegio de México, 1943.

Apogeo y decadencia del positivismo en México, Vol. II, Mexico: El Colegio de México, 1944.

En torno a una filosofía americana. Mexico: El Colegio de México, 1945.

Esquema para una historia del pensamiento en México. Lima, 1946.

Ensayos sobre filosofía en la historia. Mexico: Editorial Stylo, 1948.

Dos etapas del pensamiento en Hispanoamérica: Del romanticismo al positivismo. Mexico: El Colegio de México, 1949.

INDEX

DATE DUE